THE VILLAGE GIRL

MY DREAM, LIFE AND LEGACY

MARY WANGARI

With Dr.Kirimi Barine

Foreword by:

DR.JAMES MWANGI | **CBS CEO, EQUITY GROUP**

THE VILLAGE GIRL: My Dream, Life and Legacy

Published by;

PUBLISHING
Institute of Africa

P.O. Box 16458,
00100 NAIROBI
KENYA
info@publishing-institute.org
www.publishing-institute.org

ISBN: 978-6699-69-075-3

Note that this book contains real-life events and stories of actual people that the author has encountered. The author has taken great care to present the stories with sensitivity and respect, and to accurately portray the experiences of the individuals involved. Any negative portrayals are not intentional and are regretted.

To Mum

Time has passed, and the seasons have changed. The void you left will never be filled, but we hold on to the memories of your love and the indelible mark you left in our lives. I treasure all your lessons on integrity, focus, hard work and determination to make a better for myself. We love you and miss you dearly.

To Joy, Jackie and Lisa

I have watched you grow into beautiful, mature, responsible and intelligent young women. Mama is proud of you. I could not have asked for a better family.

When you make loving others the story of your life, there's never a final chapter, because the legacy continues. You lend your light to one person, and he or she shines it on another and another and another. And I know for sure that in the final analysis of our lives- when the to-do lists are no more, when the frenzy is finished when our e-mail inboxes are empty - the only thing that will have any lasting value is whether we've loved others and whether they've loved us.

Oprah Winfrey

Contents

Foreword

When Mary Wangari, my colleague and Group Executive Director, asked me to write the foreword for her autobiography, I was deeply honored.

Over the last two decades, Mary and I have worked closely together in various capacities.

She is an intelligent individual who can be relied on to execute tasks professionally and with great precision.

You can, therefore, imagine my predicament when she entrusted me with the responsibility of writing the foreword; the shoe was on the other foot as I have always depended on her for details and execution.

Mary's autobiography is a story of purpose and passion in her personal and professional life.

Through her unwavering commitment and devotion, she demonstrates the power of determination in the path to success. Mary is an embodiment of responsibility and accountability, the very values she has lived by all her life.

Before reading Mary's autobiography, one might think she only lives for Equity Group.

But after reading her story, one realizes that her influence extends beyond the corporate world. She has dedicated her life to serving others, beginning with God, her family, and the larger community.

In her book, Mary generously shares her wealth of experience and knowledge, which will benefit readers greatly.

The book highlights how our exposure, experiences, values, character, and pursuit of purpose are critical on our path to success.

Mary's story is a powerful reminder of the importance of diversity and inclusion in helping women to take their rightful place in society.

Her success goes to show we can overcome the biggest obstacles by refusing to be victims of the circumstances we find ourselves in.

I am immensely grateful to Mary for her enormous contribution to Equity Group and for her gift of friendship and partnership over the last 20 years.

She has significantly contributed to Equity's success and the rise of women in the Group as well as the larger society. Her story is truly inspiring and offers valuable lessons and insights that we can all learn from.

Dr. James Mwangi, CBS
Group Managing Director And CEO

Equity Group Holdings Plc

Acknowledgements

Some people greatly inspire others without knowing it, and I regret not telling you this in person. During my formative years and into adulthood I have been greatly mentored and inspired by many whom this is their calling. I learnt many lessons in church, the faith based schools I attended and this nurtured me to be the individual I am today.

I'm especially indebted to the following among many spiritual leaders I encountered: priests, deacons, sisters and specifically the Archbishop of the Catholic Archdiocese of Nyeri, His Grace Anthony Muheria and the Bishop of the Catholic Diocese of Murang'a His Lordship James Maria Wainaina. Your guidance, prayers and support and courage to speak against evils in society and lift the underprivileged in our midst has greatly inspired my journey. You are the compass that I constantly use to set my direction to the True North. I thank God for you.

A special thank you also to Fr JB Gichuhi, Fr Reuben Njagi, Fr Moses Kagunya, Fr Herman Kiboi, Fr George Gathara, Fr John Mwai, Fr Patrick Kariuki, Dr Anthony Munene, Fr Martin Ndegwa, Reverend Canon Josphat Gakuya, Bishop Charles Kariuki, Fr John Muturi and many other shepherds whose wise counsel has shaped my value system and character.

I'm grateful to everyone who encouraged me to actualise the dream of writing about the story of my life. Some gave me ideas on the title and reviewed the book, while others gave invaluable testimonials and comments that helped enrich it. The list is not exhaustive, but these include: Wambui Maina, Sr Rose Catherine Wakibiru, Catherine Nyambura, Virginia Wanjiru, Nelson Mwai, Yvonne Miteka, Hannah Njoroge, Catherine Musakali, Lucy Irungu, Mathew Ngenda, Maurice Kingori, Edwin Mwangi, Dennis Njau, Edwin Mwangi, Martin Njuguna, George Marenya, and Nick Mararo. When I became lazy and lost momentum on developing content for the book, the persistent pestering by many of you and the need to share progress, inspired me to keep at it. The very constructive and honest feedback from many of you, as I wrote, was very helpful in staying the course.

I cannot forget to thank my colleagues at Equity Group for believing in me. Your support inspires me to be a better leader. I especially, want to most sincerely thank my great mentor and the person who taught me the value of living a purposeful life and inspired me to be a better leader every day: Dr James Mwangi, who is also my Group Chief Executive Officer. You taught me how to scale the heights with boldness and courage and demonstrated how success follows a purpose-led initiative.

To my colleagues - Directors on the Equity Boards led by our Group Chairman Professor Isaac Macharia, and Executive Management of Equity Group and Subsidiaries, I say thank you. Your faith and belief in my leadership has challenged me everyday to stay on "top of things". The knowledge and wisdom you exude is inspiring to me and has shaped me to be what I am today.

A very special thank you to my support team in the Bank - Catherine Maina, Alex Muhia, Lydia Kiburu, Charity Njiru, Emma Wasilwa, Helen Njoroge, Elizabeth Owano, Lydia Ndirangu, Hellen Njiru, Ambrose Ngari, Simon Munyoike, Florence Muthama, Charity Munyori, Samuel Kirubi, Gerald Warui, Hannington Namara, Celestin Muntuabu, Isabella Maganga, Anthony Kituuka, Victor Omondi, Stephen Muendo, John Njenga, Oscar Kituyi, Christine Browne and all executives at the Group and subsidiaries for always being there and keeping things going well.

To all EQUIP Girls and all my mentees, thank you for your encouragement. I have learnt more from you than you have learnt from me through your comments, questions and very incisive feedback. You have always challenged me to put my best foot forward.

Edwin Mwangi and the Flame mentors (and 'That Group' Naomi Muthoni, Mary Catherine Wanjiku, Dennis Nyawira, Wambui Maina and Allan, Watson Muturi and Rachel, Munuhe Ng'enda and Maureen, Nelson Mwai, Ian and Waweru Irungu) you have challenged me on the need to give back and reminded me constantly that to whom much is given much will be expected. I appreciate all the insightful debates over the years and the gifts of the books, which have enriched my knowledge and wisdom. More importantly, I am grateful for becoming my second family.

A special Thank You to my extended family, including Sophia, Mathew, Dominic, Edward and Edwin together with your loving families, for your input and encouragement. I cannot forget the entire Matteo Ng'enda family and the wider Makara Ng'enda family for teaching me the basics of life in my formative years and continuing to be my cheerleaders.

A big thank you to Jackson Biko, Dr James Mwangi, Mwema Ndungo, Wambui Maina, Nelson Mwai, Shaka Kariuki, Thomas Gitahi, Dr Beth Waweru, Dr William Muraah and Samuel Kiragu for your detailed review, commentaries, editing, proofreading and invaluable feedback.

My story could not have been told without the firm shoulders of Jemimah Kiarie, Rosa Nduati-Mutero, Josephine Namasaka, Julia Kariuki, Felistus Njoroge, Veronica Mbugua Waweru, Mukami Muthee, Esther Mwangi, Jane Nyamuringa, Hon Justice SCK Isaac Lenaola, Hon Rebecca Miano MBS, William Maema, Hon Justice CA Francis Tuiyott, Hannah Waitherero, Nyokabi Mundia, Carol Musyoka, Samuel Kiragu, Ngugi Mwangi, Chege Kariuki, Grace Mugo, Nelson Waweru, Mathew & Maryanne Mwangi, Emma and James Ndoria, Colonel Lawrence Kuria & Rahab Maina, Daniel Kibuchi, Allan Gichuhi, Geoffrey Gitau and Esther Muiru among many great friends. May you all be blessed together with your loved ones.

Much appreciation to my childhood friends from the village, including Rosemary Mugechi, Catherine Wandeto, Mary Wambui Ndirangu and Thomas Gitahi together with your loving families. I cherish the memories of the fun we had growing up in the village.

The Maranga Wamae Family under the leadership of our Matriarch Margaret Maranga and the extended Wamae Kirocho family, thanks for your support and friendship.

Nick Mararo…thanks for nudging me on , for the English grammar corrections and additions. Your mastery of the English language challenges me to visit the dictionary more often.

And Clifford Machoka for the marketing and distribution strategy and critique of the book design, and The Bee Wing led by Bobbi Gassy for the support on design and graphics to a unique standard.

Thank you, Dr Kirimi Barine, my Writing Coach and Publisher, for guiding me through the entire process from concept development, editing, and design and working tirelessly to get the book out in time.

Special thanks to Jacqueline Gitau, for transcribing the handwritten manuscripts, some written in the wee hours of the morning with impeccable accuracy.

To my girls, Joy Wangui, Jacqueline Wanjiru and Lisa Wambura, thank you for keeping me on my toes when I veered off course. You always give me a different perspective on life and enriched my thoughts on several issues in the book. I love you all beyond words!

Introduction

One sunny afternoon in October 2022, I glanced outside one of the windows in my sitting room, and something caught my attention.

A gentle breeze blew the bright purple flowers off the Jacaranda tree at one end of the compound, creating a blanket of purple on the grass below.

I have lived in this house since 2015 but strangely enough, I had hitherto not noticed the beauty of the tree in full bloom.

A few weeks earlier, I had finalised the concept and outline of my autobiography with my book writing project manager.

I wasn't sure I would remember most of the details of my formative years until I opened a blank page on my laptop, and the words started to flow.

But why write a book after 54 years? In retrospect, I wish I had done it earlier.

However, being a career woman in a fast-paced industry and raising my three beautiful daughters on top of other social engagements did not leave much spare time or energy to do so.

Coincidentally, the idea of writing a book came from a casual conversation that I had with one of my mentees.

After listening to some of my childhood experiences, he was convinced they would make for an exciting read.

It was all the encouragement I needed. In our subsequent meetings, the first thing he would ask was: "How many chapters have you done so far?"

The pressure kept on mounting, and I finally started giving serious thought to the idea of documenting my story.

Also, at the beginning of 2021, I had become more active on social media, and some of the comments from my followers said being a public figure, they found my story inspiring. They encouraged me to record it for posterity.

It is against this backdrop that I write this book. I do it in the hope that it will inspire someone to aspire for a better future for themselves and their loved ones, to live a life of purpose, to want to create a legacy in their own way, to overcome failure and to refuse to quit even in the face of untold difficulties and challenges.

This is a story of a simple village girl from Tetu in Central Kenya, who rose to the top echelon of Kenya's banking industry against all odds in a space hitherto dominated by men.

The story of a girl born to a single peasant mother, whose first visit to the big city was when she joined university in the late 80s, refusing to let her past dictate her future.

A story of hope against seemingly insurmountable obstacles, dealing with the grief of losing my beloved mother, who single-handedly raised my five siblings and I, as well as coping with the painful ending of a 25-year marriage.

The story is a demonstration that with a heart full of love and a spirit as fierce as a warrior, we can wear our difficult past and hardships as armour to build a successful future.

The story also highlights the simple joys of life and the lessons I have picked up along the way, which I hope to pass on to the next generation, including helping them to use their God-given talents to excel in their professional and personal lives.

Having the boldness of spirit to conquer our greatest fears and realise our full potential in life, spurred by a strong sense of purpose to achieve dreams that may seemingly be out of reach.

One day on a flight to Kinshasa, another passenger wondered why I had opted for a vegetarian meal, declining most of the perks that come with flying business class.

They could not understand how I could turn down the fine wines on offer, the sweet-laden desserts or how I could take my coffee without sugar.

"What makes you happy?" posed the passenger exasperatedly. It got me thinking: "What truly makes me happy?"

I realised at that very moment that true happiness does not come from having the best things for ourselves but from positively impacting other people's lives through small acts of kindness and giving our time and resources to the service of others.

We are reminded of the importance of giving in 2 Corinthians 9:7-8; "Each of you should give what you have decided in your heart to give, not reluctantly or under compulsion, for God loves a cheerful giver. And God is able to bless you abundantly, so that in all things at all times, having all that you need, you will abound in every good work."

It is a reminder that when challenges knock the wind out of our sails, we have to pick ourselves up and try again. When we hit the water, we just make sure we swim to the shore. Fortune, as they say, favours the brave.

Writing about my life journey has allowed me to answer the question: "Who Am I?"

I welcome you to join me on this journey! Read on!

TRACING MY HERITAGE

01

*"Those who would judge us merely by the heights
we have achieved would do well to remember the
depths from which we started"*

Kwame Nkrumah

Nestled between the Aberdare Forest and imposing Mt Kenya, Tetu Constituency in Nyeri County is a rustic wind-swept locale famed for being the birthplace of the Mau Mau struggle.

It is best known for its famous son, Dedan Kimathi, the legendary Mau Mau general who led the armed military struggle against the British colonial regime in Kenya in the 1950s until his capture in 1956 and consequent execution in 1957.

Tetu is also the home of the 2004 Nobel Peace Laureate and area Member of Parliament between 2002 and 2007, the late Prof Wangari Maathai.

It is a land of rolling hills dotted with tea and coffee farms as well as a host of food crops such as maize and beans.

In the 50s, Tetu's rich history was entrenched, becoming the gateway through which the white man entered Nyeri County before his insidious rule spread to the rest of Central Kenya.

It is from Tetu in 1902 that British maverick Col Richard Meinertzhagen mounted a murderous campaign against locals, taking their livestock by force.

I was born here five years after independence on July 7, 1968 at Mununga-ini village on the slopes of Mt Kenya.

Across the ridge from my home is Nyeri Hill, dwarfed by the majestic snow-capped Mt Kenya (Kirinyaga) on the horizon.

The name Kirinyaga loosely translates to "place of the ostrich," but in the context of the mountain, it was used to mean "mountain of whiteness" probably because of the snow on top.

The Gikuyu believed their God, Mwene Nyaga, lived on the mountain, hence its reverence by the community. Loosely translated, it means "owner of the ostrich," but in the context of the deity, it was taken to mean "owner of the dazzling light."

Located six kilometres East of Nyeri Town and at 1,260 metres above sea level, Nyeri Hill is one of the notable landmarks within the larger Nyeri County.

On a clear sunny day, Mt Kenya can be seen from my home, a few scattered clouds hugging the contours of the mountain ridge as the crisp morning air sways the leaves of the trees in the forest below.

Sunrises and sunsets here are a sight to behold. Growing up, it was something I took for granted but which I have come to appreciate with age.

It is where the story of my life was first written by my mother, Cornelia Wanjiru Matteo, on that cold July morning when she welcomed me into the world, naming me "Maria" Wangari in keeping with her strong Catholic convictions.

A strong-willed woman, my mother had a profound impact on my life and that of my five siblings.

Despite being a single mother of six - two girls and four boys - she spared no effort to make sure we had a good start in life, which shaped our personalities to become successful individuals in our respective fields against all odds.

According to information available on the Tetu Catholic Parish website, four Consolata missionaries arrived in Kikuyu land on June 20, 1902 and were received by Chief Karuri of Tuthu in Murang'a.

The four missionaries were Father Thomas Gays, Father Fillipo Perlo, Brother Celeste Lusso and Brother Luigi Falda.

Father Thomas would later travel further north and arrive in Tetu on October 2, 1902. This was against Chief Karuri's warning that whites were not welcome in the Tetu region, where many of them had met their deaths at the hands of hostile locals.

But Father Thomas was received with open arms and is one of the early missionaries credited with the birth and growth of the Catholic Church in Tetu and later the larger Nyeri administrative area.

My maternal grandparents were among the first local people to embrace the Catholic faith, which they inculcated in their children, including my mother.

My late grandfather Ng'enda Makara was especially proud of his baptism name Matteo.

In keeping with the family tradition, I was baptised when I was only a few days old at the Mununga-ini Catholic Mission.

Growing up, my siblings and I had a normal childhood, characteristic of village life in post-colonial Kenya.

I have five siblings. My sister Sophia Kirigo is the eldest of them and is 10 years my senior.

I looked up to her when I was growing up. She always encouraged me to work hard and pass my exams.

She attended Federal High School (now Federal Academy) before joining the Kilimambogo Teachers Training College after a short stint as an untrained teacher at Ngoru Secondary School. Thereafter, she got married to Elias Kayanda, and they settled at Kiambugi, Gaturi location in Murang'a County. They are blessed with three children Githaiga, Wanjiru and Makara and several adorable grandchildren.

I loved visiting her and the family, especially during the mango season when the fruits would literally fall on your head as you sheltered from the hot afternoon sun. They are the sweetest mangoes I have ever tasted.

Sophia recently retired from her teaching job and engages in farming and other businesses with the support of her husband of over 40 years.

Mathew Ng'enda (Matteo) is our eldest brother, with six years between us. From an early age, Matteo had a knack for getting into trouble. One time, he insulted a teacher in primary school. When the news reached my Mum, he got the beating of his life.

We still laugh about it when we remember how my Mum tied him to a goat pen amid pleas for forgiveness, but she would have none of it. She caned him to a point the rest of us thought he would die.

"So you have insulted the teacher? You think the teacher is your age mate?" screamed my Mum as she whacked him with a freshly plucked cane.

By the time the beating stopped, we had all scampered for safety, fearing Mum would turn her wrath on the rest of us.

The incident is still etched in my mind. It taught me the vital lesson of always respecting my elders and those in authority.

Matteo attended Karima Boys' High School before proceeding to Njiiri School for his A-levels and consequently to Kenyatta University.

After graduation, he worked at Kenya Tea Development Agency (KTDA) and thereafter the Wood Foundation, a non-profit organization that focuses on supporting farmers in Africa.

He helped to successfully set up tea growing in southern Tanzania and also parts of Rwanda.

Matteo is my mentor and big brother, whom I turn to for advice during difficult times.

My siblings and I will forever be grateful to him for aptly filling the void of not having a father figure when growing up.

Matteo successfully brokered an out-of-court settlement over a protracted land dispute between my uncles and my Mum, cementing his place as a peacemaker in the family. He lives in Murang'a with his wife Mary Njeri. Their three sons - Murimi, Muturi, and Munuhe - are all grown up now. They call themselves the 5Ms.

My immediate older brother Dominic Makara was my partner in crime when we were young.

He would nick pancakes and other goodies from the kitchen and hide behind the toilet to enjoy his loot. Many times, I would catch him red-handed, and he would buy my silence by sharing the loot.

Makara works at KTDA and lives in Murang'a with his family. His wife Vivian has borne him two beautiful daughters Angel and Shylyn.

My younger brother Edward Theuri went to Nyeri High School and later the University of Nairobi to study Economics. He is also a qualified accountant.

Theuri briefly worked at Serena Hotel in Nairobi before he was poached by the United Nations office in Nairobi and was later seconded to Geneva, where he works and lives with his wife Schola and their children Mitchell, Trey and Jeremy.

Theuri is the epitome of reflective wisdom, a man of few words but always ready to lend a hand when required.

Edwin Kibaara is our last born. He is what you would describe as the life of the party.

His happy-go-lucky attitude and likeable demeanour makes him fun to be around. He is the official family photographer during events and is always cracking people up. Kibaara is a businessman with a nose for a good deal. He lives in Nairobi with his wife Mercy and their children Dennis, Collins, Faith, Maxwell and Wangari.

My siblings are my biggest support system and I count myself lucky to have them in my life. Each one of them has contributed to shaping my journey towards success.

—●••●—

Being a single mother, my mother assumed the role of chief disciplinarian. There were no exceptions when it came to house chores or farm work for either gender.

Everyone had to carry their own weight, and any dissent would be snuffed out in an instant.

Away from school, the house chores and back-breaking farm work kept us occupied. One of the chores I loathed the most was delivering milk to the village dairy.

My siblings and I took turns delivering the milk to the collection centre before heading to school. We would wake up as early as 3 am to make sure we were at the centre on time.

I credit this routine with making me an early riser; My day usually starts at 4.45 am, and I'm always in the office by 7 am.

I hated the coffee harvesting season, the peak of which was during the December holidays, just before Christmas.

One time, I was shuffling through the coffee bushes, picking up the red cherries when something cold and slithery brushed against my arm.

On realising it was a snake, I nearly jumped out of my skin as I ran screaming to where my Mum and my siblings were.

I turned in time to see the equally startled mûrarû (green snake) slither away into a nearby bush.

The snake, though harmless, was believed to jump into people's noses if provoked. The experience only served to strengthen my hatred for picking coffee.

After a long day on the farm, we would carry the coffee cherries to the nearby factory where there would be long queues at the quality control and weighing points.

It was not uncommon to have people spend the entire night waiting to complete the process, sometimes amid heavy downpours.

Being peasant farmers, we did not have much growing up, but my mother made sure we never went to bed hungry.

There was always enough to eat from our sizable farm where we grew bananas, maize, beans, potatoes, sweet potatoes and fruits such as passion, loquats, guavas, plums and avocados. We also kept cows, goats and chickens and also grew coffee on our farm.

My mother did not go very far with her schooling because of the lack of school fees and the upheaval caused by the Mau Mau uprising against the British.

My uncle Nderitu Matteo was given priority to go to school and would go on to become the Mayor of Nyeri town. Despite missing the opportunity to further her education, my mother was a firm believer in educating her children. I am convinced that if she had received formal education to higher levels she would have become a top CEO or administrator.

—◆•◉•◆—

The evening sun casts long shadows over Kamakwa shopping centre, a whirlwind sweeping through the dusty market as women tidy up for the day.

At one corner of the now near-empty market, a team of technicians is busy setting up their equipment on a rickety makeshift platform below a white canvas projector screen.

A few metres away, a group of children and gawky youths are huddled together, speaking in hushed tones, unable to contain their excitement.

As darkness envelopes the market, the faint stutter of the generator followed by a sharp ray of light as the first images are projected on the white canvas sends the crowd into a frenzy.

Soon everyone settles down on the dewy grass to enjoy the movie of the day, one of the many open-air cinemas that villagers would be treated to over the December holiday season.

A few minutes into the engrossing Jesus film, a projectile from the back of the crowd swishes through the air before landing smack on the back of the head of one of the older boys.

Before he knows what hit him, another one comes flying over my head, missing me by a whisker before landing on a startled man with a thud.

Then the foul smell of rotten eggs (*mathayo*) pervades the entire place as a group of boys seated at the back of the crowd bursts out laughing at the result of their naughty act.

The victims curse under their breath before wiping off the mess and turning their attention back to the movie as the culprits stifle more laughter.

This was just one of the many shenanigans that spiced up the mobile cinema events synonymous with many rural set-ups in the 80s and 90s.

They were the highlights of our school holidays after a long day on the farm.

The village also occasionally organised dance competitions, but my siblings and I were not allowed to attend those as my Mum deemed them too lewd for our age.

School holidays also provided us with the perfect opportunity to interact with our agemates of both genders.

A group of us would get together and make a rota of sorts. We would team up and till one of our parent's land before moving on to the next.

The "marathon" tilling sessions were fun as we shared our dreams and hopes for the future.

The interactions also nurtured relationships with the opposite sex, some of which ended up in marriage.

When not working on our farm or at Uncle Nderitu's, where my siblings and I helped out for a few shillings that went towards our schooling, I would visit my Aunt, Maria Wangari, Maria Wangari, at Ithenguri, a village near the border between modern-day Nyeri Municipality and Tetu Division. Auntie Maria was the oldest sibling on my mother's side. I had a soft spot for her as I was named after her under the Kikuyu customs.

During my visits, I enjoyed the company of my cousins, most of whom were my agemates.

We would work on the farm for the better part of the day but still find time to play our favourite games.

Back then, we did not have to worry about the insecurity characteristic of today's society.

We would freely roam the nearby forest, foraging for wild fruits.

Another highlight of my youth was visiting my late cousin Karu Wairagu, especially during the December holidays. He kept pigs on his farm and occasionally slaughtered one whenever he had visitors.

I usually looked forward to eating *ngarango* (a crunchy, pan-fried fatty cut of pork).

My aunt's children and I would gorge ourselves on this delicacy only to regret it later. After bingeing on it for the better part of the day, we would make a beeline for the pit latrine amid groans and heaves.

My nieces and nephews would sometimes invite their friends from the neighbourhood for a swim at a nearby river. Here, I had my first encounter with the whirligig beetle, locally known as *njururi* because of how it swims rapidly in circles on the surface of still or slow-moving water and dives when alarmed.

Legend has it that if teenage girls allow the insect to bite their undeveloped nipples, they will grow a full bust in no time. I bust this myth since even after bearing the pain and inflammation that came with the bite, I did not experience a miraculous growth of my bust. Neither do I know any girl to date who did.

My Mum and Aunt Maria were seasoned storytellers. In the evenings as we waited for supper to get ready, they would regale us with folktales, each with a lesson. Sometimes they would recount their harrowing experiences during the Mau Mau War. One of my favourite stories was that of the hare and the tortoise. It went something like this:

Once upon a time, there lived a hare. The hare could run very fast and took great pride in its speed. One day, the hare saw the tortoise walking very slowly on the road. The hare laughed at the tortoise, saying: "You are such a slowcoach, my dear friend," said the tortoise. "You are so proud of your speed. Let's have a race and see who wins." So all the animals in the forest gathered for the race. They were sure that the hare would be the clear winner. So the race started. The hare ran very fast, raising a cloud of dust in its wake. After a while, the hare turned back to check where the tortoise was. It could see the tortoise walking slowly down the road. "The tortoise will take ages to reach this point," the hare thought. And so the hare decided to take a nap after helping itself to some lush grass by the roadside. After a while, it fell into a deep slumber. Meanwhile, the tortoise edged closer with every step. It silently passed the sleeping hare. The hare suddenly jumped up from its slumber only to see the tortoise edging towards the finish line. The hare dashed it, but it was too late. The tortoise had already crossed the finish line. It could not hide its disappointment and shame after all the bragging.

"What is the moral of the story?" my Mum would ask us rhetorically as she set the dinner plates before us.

"Do not be overconfident. It breeds complacency and makes you take things for granted. It also makes you not prepare adequately and ignore important details," she would exclaim before any of us said anything.

◆•••◆

Back in the 80s, the Easter holidays were special for one reason - the Safari Rally. The rally was another highlight of my chequered childhood.

First held in 1953 as a celebration of the coronation of Queen Elizabeth 11, the event was part of the World Rally Championship from 1973 until 2002. It, however, took a 19-year hiatus, returning in 2021.

It is historically regarded as one of the toughest events in the World Rally Championship calendar, and one of the most popular rallies in Africa.

We lived for the thrill of watching the cars make their way through the muddy, winding roads near my village.

We used to wake up as early as midnight to line up along the rally route, long before the roar of the engines would be heard from miles away.

Legendary Kenyan driver Shekha Mehta was always a crowd favourite. Locals would cheer him as he navigated the muddy terrain with his Datsun car.

The simplicity of village life is something that I miss to this day. I could not trade my childhood and youth spent in the village for the many comforts the children of today enjoy.

If I could do it all over again, I would choose the village 10 times over. It shaped me into the person I am today.

◆•••◆

One of my second cousins, Raphael Makara, was the only other person apart from the village shopkeeper Barnabas to own a car in my village.

His car became an ambulance of sorts, ferrying expectant mothers and gravely ill patients to the hospital.

Makara was always at hand to drive someone to the hospital whenever called upon.

Occasionally, some women would give birth in the car. Home births were also common at the time, with the village midwives attending to those who were unable to make it to the hospital on time.

Those who gave birth in hospitals would be presented with a gift hamper containing towels, baby shawls, Cusson's baby soaps and oils and other provisions like baby food.

This acted as an incentive for women to deliver in the hospital instead of enlisting the services of village midwives.

Back then, most mothers breastfed their children until the next one was born. It was not uncommon for a two-year-old child to walk up to their mother and demand *"nyonyo"* (the breast).

Feeding bottles were a rarity. A majority of mothers fed their children roast bananas, which they would chew and spit into a spoon or their hands and stuff into the baby's mouth.

This was an alternative to blenders, which are a common feature in many modern homes today.

This feeding method was not exclusive to mothers. If another woman or an older sibling had to babysit, they would do the same.

When it came to sleeping arrangements in the village, we did not have modern-day mattresses.

Most households had single spring beds. The mattresses were made of straw. Due to limited space and resources, three to four people would share a bed.

Woe unto you if one of your siblings wet the bed. All of you would wake up the following morning smelling of urine. Other bedding such as pillows and bed sheets was unheard of.

A blanket or two sufficed. One of the downsides of a spring bed was that most of them were not designed to support the weight of four people and tended to sag in the middle due to uneven distribution of weight.

We would end up sleeping on top of each other or sink to the ground whenever one of the springs snapped.

With time, spring beds were replaced by wooden beds that had leather straps in the middle.

And since most mothers were full-time housewives, they took their children with them everywhere, including the farm.

They would put their nursing babies under a tree as they worked, stopping at intervals to feed them.

Back then, diapers and nappies for babies were a preserve of the well-heeled. Adults too had to improvise when it came to toilet hygiene. The natural toilet paper of the time was *maigoya*, scientifically known as Plectranthus barbatus.

Known as the traditional toilet paper, the plant's soft and broad leaves made for a good substitute for toilet paper. Many households planted the plant near the pit latrines or would pluck the leaves elsewhere and stack them up nearby for anyone visiting the "little room."

If one homestead ran out of stock, it was common to "borrow" a few leaves from their neighbour's compound. Talk of the good old days!

A JOURNEY OF DISCOVERY

02

"If your dreams do not scare you, they are not big enough".

Ellen Johnson Sirleaf

From a tender age, I had a burning desire to join school, go to university, get a good job and later help my Mum financially. I was barely five when I decided I could not wait to go through nursery school before joining primary school.

"I want to go to school, Mum", I told her one morning. "You know you must go to nursery school first before you can join the main school", she responded, rolling her eyes dismissively.

Back then, one had to pass the "ear test" to join Class One. You were required to touch your left ear with your right hand, passing over the middle of the head to pass the test. It was a rather archaic way of limiting the number of those joining primary school as it had nothing to do with one's intellect. Intelligent but small-bodied pupils were locked out from progressing to Class One, some for several years, while more physically endowed individuals would be pushed through.

I kept on pestering my Mum until one day, she agreed to take me to see the head teacher, the late Mr Simon Wambugu, who agreed to give me an audience, perhaps out of sheer amusement that someone who had not yet been through nursery school let alone passing the "ear test" wanted to join Class One.

As expected, I failed the test. "See, I told you. You are not ready to join school yet", my Mum teased me. "Tell them to give me another test, and I will prove them wrong", I shot back on the verge of tears. My mother happened to be a member of the school committee, so I was given another hearing to make my case. The committee administered a written and oral test, both of which I aced despite not having any form of formal schooling.

And thus began the academic journey that would take me to places I never thought possible for a simple village girl like me. And I loved school! Wearing the royal blue tunic made of thin cotton material with orange collars every morning of the school term and making a dash for school was one of the most fulfilling things I have done in life.

"Úngienda gûthoma, primary school, wambe uthîî nursery ugîe meciria. Teacher nî mwarimû, chair nî gîtî, window nî ndirica, arm nî guoko." (If you want to go to primary school, go to nursery school first and sharpen your brain. *Mwarimû* is a teacher, *gîtî* is a chair, *ndirica* is a window and *guoko* is an arm). That's how I learnt the white man's language!

The irony of this popular nursery school rhyme was not lost on me when I joined Class One in that I actually skipped the class. The night before my first day at school, I could hardly sleep.

I was up before dawn and excitedly put on my uniform, ready to conquer the world. The rest of the day was a whirlwind of activity. I soon got into the routine of school life. I would look forward to the morning walks to school with my agemates and the leisurely trot back home in the afternoon.

In school, we learnt many life skills, including sweeping the earthen floor, pottery and sewing, the latter of which was part of the curriculum. Turns out the recently introduced Competency-Based Curriculum (CBC) in Kenya's education system is nothing new!

Meanwhile, I immersed myself in schoolwork. I particularly loved maths and became so good at it that my teachers would have me tutor other pupils.

Away from class, we never missed an opportunity to have fun, sometimes too much of it that we got into trouble. During break time once, another girl and I were competing to see who would cross from one end of the goalpost to the other without falling. When it was my turn, I started clambering across the rough horizontal metal rod. Midway through, I lost grip and came tumbling with a thud! I imagine that's what happens to a "Tomboy" with a girl's name!

The other pupils could not help bursting into laughter instead of comforting me. Luckily, I did not break any bones, but I was sore for several days from the fall. I, however, would not dare mention it to my Mum, lest I got the beating of my life.

Besides insistence on academic excellence, most teachers were sticklers for rules. They taught us basic values, such as the importance of respect for elders and those in authority. Discipline was also emphasised at our local church, Mununga-ini Catholic Mission, with some elders acting as chaperones in social gatherings to enforce the church's stance on chastity and morality.

Back then, one did not have to be your parent or close relative to discipline you. If an older person caught you misbehaving, they would mete out instant punishment, including caning, a pinch on the cheeks or in extreme cases, a slap. And it did not stop there. They would take it upon themselves to report you to your parents, who would administer their own punishment.

Looking back, that kind of punishment system was an effective deterrent to childhood delinquency, which today has gotten out of hand. From an early age, I devoted myself to a life of prayer and service to the church.

I was a member of the Catholic Action Group. The group focused on teaching principles of the Catholic faith by encouraging the faithful to serve others through prayer, giving alms, community service and evangelism. This gave me a solid foundation in the Catholic faith. I had a great time with my childhood friends, including Rosemary Mugechi Catherine Wandeto and Mary Wambui Ndirangu attending the Easter vigils at our church. As Catholic girls, we had a great time when we attended the Easter vigils at our church and joined other Christians for an evening of prayer and reflection.

Catholic Action was established by Pope Pius XI (1922-1933) when the church felt threatened by the ideologies of communism and socialism. Catholic missionaries arrived in Kenya at the turn of the early 20th century, seeking to popularise the new religion ahead of other competing interests by Western colonial governments.

At home, every evening, we would pray the rosary together before dinner and recite prayers from *Gatabu ka Mahoya* (the Gĩkũyũ prayer book).

In many rural homes in the 70s and 80s, families would cook and eat their meals from detached kitchens. The children would sit around the fireplace as mothers prepared the evening meal. The fireplace was strictly the mother's territory and consisted of three stones over which the pot would be placed to cook over a fire powered by firewood while the older folks regaled the younger generation with tales of the Mau Mau war or simply taught them about their culture.

It provided an opportunity for the family to bond without the distractions of modern-day society.

We did not have a TV when I was growing up. Our only news source was the family's transistor radio, which only aired Voice of Kenya (VoK), the national broadcaster, with programming running from 5 pm-10 pm. The first time I watched TV was when I joined secondary school. The TV, which was stationed in the dining room, would only be switched on during weekends.

I also wore my first pair of shoes in high school, courtesy of one of my aunties, who bought them for me for passing well in my Certificate for Primary Education (CPE). The exam was administered by the Kenya National Examinations Council (KNEC), and the highest score was 36 points, of which I scored 34.

My Mum encouraged me to study hard, constantly reminding me that only a good education would help me escape the drudgery of village life. "You have no other networks to save you from this life", she would say, noting that it was within my power to determine the kind of life I wanted to create for myself.

I took Mum's words to heart, and my hard work paid off. I sat my CPE in 1980 at Tetu Boys' Primary School, scoring the highest marks ever by any pupil at the school then! Yes, I graduated from a "boys' primary school." The backstory of how I ended up at a boys' school is an interesting historical fact.

And no one found it more amusing than my new classmates at Kangubiri Girls' High School, a former detention camp converted into a girls' boarding school after independence. The school's name, in Tetu Constituency, Nyeri County, was coined from the last line before detainees were released and the white colonists declared the detainees can "can go free".

During the first class, after admission to the school, the class teacher asked everyone to introduce themselves and state their former primary school. When my turn came, I stood up and confidently said: "I am Mary Wangari from Tetu Boys' Primary School".

Everyone burst out laughing. "What?" asked the class teacher, who thought I was trying to be funny amid another burst of laughter from the other girls. "I am Mary Wangari from Tetu Boys' Primary School," I repeated feebly, my confidence now having deserted me.

It was at this point that it hit me why everyone was in stitches; they could not wrap their minds around how a girl would be admitted to a boys' school. Some even questioned my gender.

"Are you serious, you attended a boys' school?" asked the class teacher incredulously.

"Not exactly, teacher", I answered.

"How did that happen?" she probed further.

So, I set on explaining how Tetu Boys' School ended up admitting girls while retaining its former name. When the missionaries came to Tetu, they opened two primary schools - Tetu Girls' Primary School and Tetu Boys' Primary School. My late grandfather Matteo Ng'enda donated the land on which the latter school was built. But due to the clamour by parents keen on avoiding paying the development levy twice if they had children in both schools, the missionaries opened admissions at Tetu Boys' to either gender.

"I guess they forgot to change the name, hence the confusion", I explained, putting to rest the speculation among some of the girls that I was a boy disguised as a girl.

In 2021, in honour of my late grandfather, the school was posthumously renamed St Matthew's Tetu Boys' Primary School. The boy's tag has refused to go away!

Life at Kangubiri was uneventful. Besides the usual emotional roller coaster of transitioning into adolescence and the initial homesickness, I settled into the routine of boarding school life pretty well. I put my head down, studied hard and participated in extracurricular activities, including music, drama, and Catholic Action.

I was part of the school choir that won the overall award at the Kenya Music Festival in the 80s under the guidance of our music teacher, Mr Gikonyo (Sorino, as we called him discreetly!). I looked forward to school trips for drama competitions and science congress events. Occasionally, we had exchange programmes with some of our neighbouring schools like Nyeri High School, Kagumo High and Tumutumu Girls'. Such events provided good "hunting grounds" for those keen on having romantic relationships with the opposite sex. I, however, kept away from the boys on my Mum's advice that *"arume me rwamba* (men sting).

Here, I made good friends like Sister Catherine Wakibiru (now a Catholic nun with Assumption Sisters of Nairobi), Beatrice Kamau, and Mercy Mukami Kabugua, among others I have kept in touch with until today.

Meanwhile, my streak of good performance in almost all subjects continued in high school, winning me several accolades and awards. I particularly loved Mathematics, Biology and Chemistry, especially the practical lab lessons.

When I joined high school, two of my brothers were also there, while my eldest sister Sophia Kirigo was in Kilimambogo Teachers Training College. With myself and two of my brothers in high school now, the financial burden for my mother only got heavier. In those days, boys' education was prioritised over that of girls. My Mum experienced the injustice of it firsthand when she was made to forfeit the chance to join Mugoiri Girls' High School in Murang'a in favour of her brothers Kibaara and Nderitu.

But this was a choice she did not have to make over the future of any of her children. Despite the strain of being a single mother, she ensured that we all got an equal chance to study and shape our dreams, irrespective of gender. Besides subsistence farming and the meagre proceeds, she got from selling some of her farm produce and the sale of coffee, she had no other constant source of income. She supplemented her earnings from tailoring and crocheting, which put us through school.

My Mum later joined forces with a group of villagers, including Justus Wagoki, Barnabas Kibugu, Muruthi Gachoya and Johana Gitahi Gachura (father of former Nation Media Group CEO Linus Gitahi now the Chairman of Diamond Trust Bank), among others, and formed an investment club by the name Mununga-ini Investment Group. They used to meet once a month and pool resources, which over time, they used to buy some land on which they put up several buildings that generate some income for them to date.

The second generation now manages the investment group under the able chairmanship of Muruthi Gachoya and my brother Mathew Ng'enda after the demise of most of our parents. Through this, she gave me a practical lesson on the need to make small savings and investments irrespective of the size of your income. I have modelled my savings and investment plans around this.

In her heydays, my mother was a dedicated community service worker. She was among the pioneering members of the Nyeri chapter of the Maendeleo ya Wanawake Organisation, which was formed in 1952. Together with other members, she is credited with spearheading a campaign to phase out grass-thatched, mud-walled houses in my village and replacing them with semi-permanent ones made of timber and tin roofs.

The lobby also spearheaded awareness of good crops and animal husbandry in the village. My Mum was among the first farmers to grow capsicum *(pilipili hoho)* in Nyeri County on a pilot basis, with her farm serving as a demonstration centre under the supervision of Agricultural officials from Wambugu Agriculture Training Centre (Wambugu Farm). Today, the Mt Kenya region is one of the leading suppliers of capsicum in the country.

Growing up in the village shaped my view on matters of money. It taught me the value of building social capital, especially when it comes to getting credit. Like in most villages even today, our local shopkeeper, Barnabas Kibugu, was key to the survival of many families. Mr Kibugu would allow families to take goods on credit and, depending on their creditworthiness, pay at the end of the week or month.

The Equity Bank agency banking model is built around this rudimentary credit access model. One of the habits I developed early on in life was to account for every penny. I would write down the cost of every item and the exact change. The cost of basic commodities at the time was quite low. Bread cost fifty cents, *unga* (maize flour) seventy cents, and sugar sixty cents.

There was no room for lying with my Mum. One day I was given some change of 10 cents coin, but I lost it on the way back home. She would hear none of it, and she made me retrace my steps and find it.

Despite my best efforts, I never found the coin. An elderly neighbour saved my skin after he offered to replace the coin, seeing my distress as I went looking for it along the road. To date, transparency in all my dealings with others, be it at a personal or professional level, is non-negotiable.

I scored a First Division of 20 points in my Kenya Certificate of Secondary Education. I wanted to specialise in the sciences (read medicine) for my "A" levels at Ngandu Girls, which was later renamed Bishop Gatimu Ngandu Girls School, but I was relegated to the Arts class. I bitterly complained to the Headmistress Ms Helen Waweru, but she would hear none of it. I had no choice but to accept to join arts class true to the saying when life hands you some lemons, make some lemonade.

Situated in Mathira, Nyeri County, it is a Catholic Church-sponsored school. I enjoyed my time there being a practising Roman Catholic. On weekends, we would go for apostolic work, including visiting the sick and elderly.

Here, I made good friends like Lucy Wangari, Josephine Sichangi, Lucy Kagwanja, and Esther Mwangi, among others, some of whom later became classmates in Law School. Catherine Wandeto, my friend from the village, also went to Ngandu though she was my junior in school.

The Italian nuns who ran the school were very strict when it came to observing the school rules and regulations. One of the sisters by the name of Sr Lucille would get emotional when releasing us on closing day, saying: "Girls, I am releasing you to the world with prayers. Do not be cheated by boys. They will make you pregnant."

I sat for my final A-level exams in 1986 and passed with flying colours. I was over the moon to be admitted to the University of Nairobi's Faculty of Law.

IN PURSUIT OF PURPOSE

03

"If you can't figure out your purpose, figure out your passion. For your passion will lead you right into your purpose".

— T.D. Jakes

I had lived all my life in my village in Nyeri before being admitted to the University of Nairobi. I had only been to the city twice before to attend the Kenya Music Festival and another time for the Nairobi Trade Fair (The Nairobi Show as it was called then). Coming to the big city was, therefore, unnerving as it was exciting.

When I received my admission letter to the University of Nairobi to study Law, I was very excited. I was not sure whether it was the opportunity to finally leave village life behind that excited me more or the prospect of becoming the first lawyer from Mununga-ini. On the eve of reporting to the university, sleep eluded me, perhaps from being anxious that I would oversleep and miss the bus.

My cousin James Wambugu had also been admitted to the university to do engineering. His Mum escorted us to Nairobi, while my elder brother Mathew Ng'enda, who was in his final year at Kenyatta University, met us at Tea Room, where public service vehicles from Nyeri terminate.

The little girl from Mununga-ini had finally landed in the big city, armed with nothing but lofty dreams of becoming a top lawyer.

Campus life was eventful and eye-opening for me, coming straight from the village. At the women's hall of residence, commonly referred to as "Box", Lady Justice Roselyn Aburili (now a judge of the High Court of Kenya) was my first roommate. We occasionally meet to reminisce on the good old days. Roselyn was a bookworm and spent most of her time in the library. No wonder she has established a distinguished career in the Judiciary!

At the time, students got full government sponsorship that took care of all their tuition and accommodation expenses and only repaid the money when they started working. Unlike today where the Higher Education Loans Board only caters for a certain percentage of these charges, our parents did not have to pay a dime! We even got a stipend every semester, popularly known as the "boom".

Many students used the money for such excesses as partying, buying the latest music systems and new clothes. I was, however, alive to my family situation back home, and instead of squandering the money, I used it to help my Mum educate my two younger brothers, Edward and Edwin, through High School.

In my second year, I moved to the famed Stella Awinja Women's Hall of Residence. Previously known as St Mary Hall, the hostel was renamed in honour of Stella Muka Awinja, a former student who died in 1984 in a freak accident when a stone fell on her while walking on the sidewalk during the construction of Lilian Towers on University Way in the Nairobi Central Business District. Stella was a third-year engineering student at the time and was also a gifted thespian and aspiring playwright.

My time at the famed dormitory came to an end in the second semester of that year when the University decided to move the Law School from the Main Campus near the Central Business District to the new Parklands Campus. The new campus was smaller, but our time there was just as enjoyable as at the Main Campus.

We had consummate lecturers in Constitutional Law, Land Law, Law of Evidence, Contract Law, Tort Law, Banking and Insurance Laws, among other subjects. The good training gave me a very good foundation for a career in private practice that I engaged in for 13 years after my admission as an advocate of the High Court of Kenya by Chief Justice Hancox in October 1991.

During my time at the University of Nairobi, I was a member of the St Paul's Catholic Chapel Community and actively participated in youth activities under the church, such as retreats and singing in the choir. This kept me grounded in an environment where a majority of the students succumbed to the peer pressure of letting their hair down away from the supervision of their parents and guardians.

Our University choir was once invited to Kabarnet Gardens - the late President Daniel Moi's Nairobi private home - to entertain his guests. Besides the privilege of entertaining the head of state and his high-profile guests, we also enjoyed the goodies that came with such a junket, including a hearty meal that we could only dream about at the time.

Away from campus, I was also a member of the Nyeri District University Student Association, a lobby that brought together university students from my region. Apart from spearheading the issues of students from the larger Nyeri district, the Association was also involved in corporate social responsibility activities. One such activity was cleaning and repainting the Karatina General Hospital. We also planned group activities, including road trips and outings, which were a lot of fun.

My first brush with the law came in the third year following the death of former Cabinet Minister Robert Ouko in unclear circumstances. The students organised a demonstration to protest the killing. The plan was to peacefully march along Uhuru Highway, calling for those responsible for the heinous act to be brought to book. Things, however, turned sour when police confronted us at the junction of Uhuru Highway and University Way, demanding we disperse immediately.

We stood our ground chanting, "who killed Ouko?" forcing the police to fire tear gas canisters in the ensuing melee. Luckily, no major casualties were reported, and the matter did not escalate, as sustained protests would have seen the university closed for a lengthy time. Such closures were synonymous with many public universities at the time, which disrupted the learning calendar.

The rest of my time at the university passed without much incident. And on a rainy morning on October 17, 1990, the graduating class assembled at the Great Court for our big day. The University had just moved the ceremony to the newly designated Graduation Square to accommodate the large number of students in the double intake class but unfortunately had not prepared the grounds in good time hence the messy muddy court.

The weather did not dampen our spirits. My immediate family and friends had arrived in a hired 25-seater matatu to cheer on the first lawyer from Mununga-ini village. My cousin Michael Alex Kamwaro was the DJ of the trip, keeping the villagers entertained throughout the trip and making them forget the misery of the matatu breaking down twice during the trip.

Unfortunately, for all the colour and pomp of the occasion, I only have one photo to mark my graduation, which we took at Ramogi Studios in downtown Nairobi after the cameraman I had hired for the day vanished into thin air with my deposit.

The homecoming party was even bigger, with the rest of the village joining the celebrations. My mother and other women could not contain their joy as they heartily sang traditional songs.

I graduated with a Second Class Honours (Upper Division) Degree, setting me up for the next stage of becoming a full-fledged lawyer by joining the Kenya School of Law for the mandatory one-year Diploma studies before being admitted to the bar.

One of the outcomes of campus life that I am excited about is the friendships for life that have continued to this day. The Law Class that graduated in 1990 formed an Alumni Association and named it MV90.

So, what is the story behind MV90?

MV90 was started in February 2017 by a number of my lady classmates at the University of Nairobi as a Whatsapp group open to the University of Nairobi law graduates of the year 1990. MV90 simply means 'motor vessel 90', a ship. Why a ship? Hon Justice Isaac Lenaola, Judge of the Supreme Court of Kenya, member and first Captain of the ship, explained to me that he coined the name to denote the fact that, in 1990, upon receiving our undergraduate degrees, we were released to the sea of life but reunited in the group like sailors on a ship sailing the deep seas united in one common goal; to succeed and thrive in life.

Group members proudly call each other Sailors, and the camaraderie in the group has borne huge successes. Called boats that are tied to the MV90 ship, the group has probably one of the most unique welfare groups. It also has an investment LLP, a Book Club, and a Farmer's Group, among other initiatives to harness the mental and financial resources of sailors/members for the common group.

What started as a typical Kenyan Whatsapp group with witty, naughty and most times serious comments has grown into a large, successful family with millions of shillings in investments and welfare but, more fundamentally, a reunited group of young men and women, who on 15th June 1987 entered the University of Nairobi as greenhorns, graduated on 22nd October 1990 and yet today straddle the Judiciary, Legal Practice, National Assembly, the Senate, the Cabinet and other Government positions, UN and other global institutions, Corporate Institutions with extreme success. I am a happy and proud sailor on MV90.

—•••—

In 1991, I was admitted as an advocate of the High Court of Kenya after the successful completion of the six-month pupillage at Muraguri & Muraguri Company Advocates in Murang'a town. The idea of working in Nairobi did not appeal to me much at the time. I wanted to stay closer home. But midway through my six-month internship journey, the company, which had another office in Nairobi, asked me to move to the city office.

The firm's managing partner, Onesmus Muraguri, informed me that a senior lawyer, Mr Muturi Kigano, who later became Kangema MP, needed an associate lawyer. I was interviewed for the position and hired on the spot.

At taking my new appointment, I found accommodation in a single room in Nairobi's Umoja Estate. The place was clearly unsafe but affordable. One night, thieves stole my neighbour's car tyres. The car would be parked right outside my window. Just the thought that whoever stole it was there as I slept and I did not hear a thing was unsettling.

The following day, I moved out to a shared bedsitter in Otiende, Lang'ata. Back then, bedsitters did not have an in-built bathroom and toilet areas. The facilities were placed outside and shared among the many tenants within the housing block. The area was notorious for an erratic supply of water, with just one tap serving the entire block. Water from the City Council would run for only an hour daily between 4 am and 5 am.

My roommate Wanjiku and I took turns waking up to fill up the assorted containers we used for storing water. There would already be a winding queue of shivering tenants waiting at the communal tap by the time we woke up. Most days, the water would run out before our turn came. Add this to the traffic nightmare on Lang'ata Road, which was yet to be expanded to dual lanes at the time, and life could not have been more difficult for area residents.

Traffic began to build up before 6 am despite there not being as many vehicles on the road at the time as there are today. It would take two hours to get to the City Mortuary roundabout, for a distance of about ten kilometres. To get to my office opposite the Prestige Plaza on Ngong Road on time meant I had to be out of the house by 6 am despite the short distance.

I moved house across the city to the South B area after only three weeks. While the house was similar to the previous one in design, its location was more convenient since transport to and from work was more accessible.

It is while I lived there that one of the life-changing events of my life took place; I conceived my first child, Joy, and got engaged to Dr Wamae Maranga, who later became my husband. Though I liked the house a lot, I had to move to a more spacious one with a baby now on the way.

My next destination in seeking convenient housing was Kabiria in Riruta Satellite, a suburb in Dagoretti South Constituency near Waithaka. Being farther from the city, life here was serene, and I made many good friends like the Githendus, among others.

My salary at the time was about Ksh5,000, which by any standard wasn't modest but not much. And considering my fiance was still in Medical School until he graduated and found work, the burden of raising our baby would squarely fall on me. I had to make some tough choices, hence the decision to move to Riruta where rent was relatively affordable. Rent for a one-bedroom house was Ksh1,500.

The bus stop was about a 30-minute walk from the house, quite a challenge for a heavily pregnant woman. I, however, devised a way out of this taxing daily routine. My next-door neighbour, Mr Odima, happened to own a car, a red Datsun 160J. He would leave his house around 7 am, so I decided to leave 10 minutes earlier and slowly begin walking to the bus stop. My plan was he would catch up with me before I walked too far and give me a lift considering my state. But alas! He did not turn up on the first day I put my clever plan in motion.

I was annoyed, as if he was obligated to give me a lift. But the following day, sure enough, Mr Odima caught up with me just as I was about to give up on my plan. He offered me a lift, and I gladly accepted. Thus began a daily routine that would see him drop me off at the bus stop before driving off. Mr Odima remained a friend even after I moved out of the estate and later became my client when I set up my private practice.

Being peri-urban, life in Riruta had a rural feel to it, and neighbours were concerned for each other, unlike today, where everybody minds their own business. Families would invite each other to events like children's birthdays and initiation ceremonies.

My daughter Joy Wangui, named after my husband's mother as per Kikuyu customs, was born in September 1992. She was closely followed by her sister, Jacqueline Wanjiru, three years later, who was named after my mum Wanjiru. By that time, we had moved to Nyayo Highrise Estate along Mbagathi Way. We stayed there until 1997, when we moved to a three-bedroom maisonette in Ngumo Estate.

Motherhood brought about a deep sense of responsibility and maturity. As a young mother, I went through the rollercoaster of sometimes feeling overwhelmed from having to balance my work, taking care of the children as well as being a wife. It is a well-known fact that career women always live in guilt of whether they were giving sufficient time and love for their children and family, and I wasn't any exception. Sometimes I wished I could have more time at home, but as they say, it is all about ensuring a work-life integration to balance all interests competing for time on the calendar.

There was also the usual disappointment of dealing with the house helps, who would walk out on you in the morning without notice as you prepared for work, leaving you to your own devices. Others would steal from you or your neighbours before escaping.

I remember one of them who would steal my neighbour's young son's clothes from the clothesline. My neighbour complained to me about her suspicion, and I decided to investigate. I was shocked to also find matchboxes, curry powder and bar soaps stashed under her bed. We settled the matter with my neighbour amicably, but I had to fire the criminal house girl on the spot.

One sunny afternoon in 2002, I was sitting in my office at Old Mutual Building in the Central Business District when the receptionist, Margaret Gathoga, tapped on the door.

"Excuse me, ma'am, there is someone here to see you," she said, glancing over at the lobby.

"Let them in," I said, looking up from the pile of documents I was poring over.

"You can come in," said the receptionist, motioning the gentleman into my office.

"Good afternoon," he said as he strode in and gave me a firm handshake.

"My name is James [Mwangi]. I am the Finance Director of Equity Building Society," he added.

"Nice to meet you, James," I replied, inviting him to have a seat.

At that time my law firm was on the panel of lawyers of Equity. He explained that he had been referred to me by one of his colleagues in the credit department, Ambrose Ngari, whom I had interacted with regularly. Ambrose is currently General Manager and the team lead at Corporate Supreme Centre.

He (James) told me he had some legal work for me. James explained that Equity Building Society had attracted a strategic investor by the name of Africap Microfinance Fund to support the company's growth strategy. The private equity fund was looking to invest $1.6 million (Ksh120 million at that time), and so Equity was looking for a lawyer to draw up the contract.

I had hitherto not handled any brief worth even a fraction of the amount, and I was terrified by James' request instead of being thrilled by the prospects of making a huge commission.

"What if something went wrong? Why would they entrust me, a little-known lawyer with such a huge deal?" I wondered in my mind.

"Why didn't he go to the more recognised law firm across the road, Kaplan & Stratton?"

I had just moved from a crumpled-up office in downtown Nairobi on Luthuli Avenue, a busy part of the city best known for counterfeit electronic goods and cosmetics. Here I was about to clinch a multi-million-shilling deal. I did my best to mask my apprehension and agreed to take the client's brief.

As soon as James was out of the building, I rushed to the High Court Library to conduct some research. The draft contract had strange terms like "put option, tag along, drag along and right of first refusal," which I needed to come to grips with. I asked the librarian, an old friend of mine called Cecilia, to give me all the books on Commercial Law and contracts that she could find.

And thus began my long relationship with Equity.

➤•••➤

After graduating from the Kenya School of Law, and subsequent admission as an Advocate of the High Court of Kenya by the then Chief Justice Allan Robin Winston Hancox, my first job was as a legal assistant at Kigano & Associate Advocates in 1991 before venturing into private practice.

I was a generalist, handling litigation, conveyance and contract law as well as landlord-tenant disputes. I also took several pro-bono cases as a way of building my profile, representing clients who could not afford a lawyer. For such cases, I had a close working relationship with organisations such as the Federation of Women Lawyers in Kenya (FIDA) and the human rights lobby, Kituo Cha Sheria.

As I grew into the profession, I was amazed at how slowly the wheels of justice could turn.

Adjudication of some cases took decades. I once came across a case that was filed in 1968, the year I was born, and it was still pending in court.

My first office was at Luthuli House on Luthuli Avenue in downtown Nairobi, a part of the city marked by a cacophony of hooting *matatus* (public transport buses), hawkers and loud music from the myriad of electronics shops that line up the street. The area was also notorious for petty thieves and hordes of street urchins looking to get a few coins from passers-by.

I experienced first-hand the harsh reality of life in this part of town after having my wristwatch snatched twice near the busy Kencom bus stop by some of the street boys who panhandle in the area.

When I started out on my own, the workspace was shared. I had a sublease agreement with a gentleman who ran a printing business and dutifully paid the agreed rent to him on the understanding that he would, in turn, pay the landlord promptly. But I was shocked one morning when auctioneers invaded my office, claiming my rent was in arrears.

Apparently, the gentleman who ran the printing business had not been remitting the rent to the landlord. I tried to plead my case with the auctioneers, but they would have none of it. And so, I decided to go see the landlord, the late Mr Stephen Kung'u, a no-nonsense businessman, who also owned the Kunste Hotel in Nakuru town.

When I was done explaining my predicament, I was taken aback by his reaction.

"You said you are a lawyer, right?" he asked incredulously, his eyes narrowing with exasperation.

"Yes," I answered in a shaky voice.

"Then I have never met one as stupid as you," he shot back. "You of all people should know that subletting office space is illegal."

I was left speechless at his last statement. After gathering my thoughts, I tried to explain to him that I was just a young lawyer starting out and could not afford a direct tenancy. After much haggling, he agreed to hold off the eviction on the condition that I would take up another space in the same building. I would, however, bear the cost of renovating the new space. From that time, Mr Kung'u became a good friend and occasionally consulted me whenever he had trouble with one of the other tenants.

After three years at Luthuli House, I could sustainably make rent for a better office and I crossed over to the third floor of the Old Mutual Building along Kimathi Street in 1999. Here good fortunes too followed and I had my first big break following the visit by James from Equity Building Society.

I had no idea how my encounter with Mr Mwangi, or James as he liked to be referred to and whom I later came to learn was a very senior figure at the banking institution, would transform my life.

➤•••➤

Following James' visit, I satisfactorily closed Equity's deal with Africap Microfinance Fund. The investors provided the money, allowing Equity Building Society to start the process of converting into a full-fledged commercial bank in 2004.

My role in the successful conclusion of the transaction earned the bank's top management confidence in the hitherto "inexperienced" lawyer. Consequently, they asked me to lead the team overseeing the transition, and in January 2005, Equity Building Society opened its doors as Equity Bank Ltd.

This was one of the significant turning points in my career. It opened the door to more engagements with the bank, including handling conveyance briefs for customers. It involved preparing loan and securities documentation before the funds could be disbursed to customers.

As the transition kicked into high gear, I was left with no time to run my law firm. I delegated most of the duties to my legal assistant, but some clients insisted on being attended to by me. I expressed this concern to Mr Mwangi, who had by this time ascended to the position of CEO.

His answer was terse: "Why don't you come on board full-time?"

It sounded simple and enticing.

It would guarantee me a steady pay cheque if I agreed to trade my spartan office in the Central Business District for an office on the 14th floor of the NHIF Building that housed Equity's offices at the time.

But how would I walk away from a business I had built from scratch for close to 10 years to a little-known Building Society? On top of that, I had no training or knowledge of banking. I did not want to make a rash decision, so I asked Mr Mwangi to give me time to think it over.

Over the next few days, I took time to re-evaluate my career goals. On the one hand, I had the opportunity of a lifetime to launch a thriving legal practice where I would be my own boss and while at it make a tonne of money. On the other hand, I was offered an opportunity to be part of a journey to transform Kenya's financial landscape.

From my initial engagement with Mr Mwangi, I was sold on Equity's business model. It was one of promoting financial inclusion with a strong social impact component. I had already started seeing the impact it was having in empowering the previously unbanked population.

Finally after lengthy consultations with my family, I said yes! And one bright morning in September 2004, I joined Equity Building Society as employee number 712.

Some of my friends thought I was crazy for moving to a hitherto unknown institution, which was not even a "bank".

◄ •••► ─

When I joined Equity Bank, it only had 18 branches, 500 employees and a balance sheet of about Ksh3 billion ($ 30 million). Among the notable employees at the time were Gerald Warui, who is currently the Managing Director of the Kenyan subsidiary, which is the largest in the Group.

Others were Alex Muhia, the Director of Communications; Catherine Maina and Charity Njiru, the Executive Assistants to the Group CEO. They helped me settle down and have over the years been a great help in my career growth. Emma Wasilwa, my Executive Assistant, came on board later and has since been with me.

After the conversion to Equity Bank Limited, we embarked on an exponential growth plan. At the time, Equity had a very weak brand presence and was silently referred to as the "Mount Kenya Bank" in some quarters, largely because of its origin in Kangema in modern-day Murang'a County.

Dr Peter Kahara Munga, who was a civil servant then, noticed that area residents, including his mother, struggled to process the payments received by cheques for farm produce like coffee, tea and milk since they had no bank accounts. They had to give all those small cheques to him to figure out how to encash them. Back then, you could endorse cheques to a third party, and fraud levels were low.

But it was a humiliating and cumbersome process that indignified the low-income savers. So, Dr Munga got some of his friends together, and they raised money and opened Equity Building Society in 1984 since licensing requirements for such a financial institution were not as strict as those for a bank that required Ksh 250 million ($2.5 million).

When Equity opened its doors as a building society, it took short-term deposits but lent longer term. But unfortunately, it also turned out that they needed more deposits and revenues to operate sustainably. The initial mortgage services model failed since there was a serious mismatch between savings and loans, and by 1991, Equity Building Society was technically insolvent and marked for closure after a Central Bank inspection. The founders pleaded for time within which to turnaround the business to profitability which they got on the condition that they overhaul the management team. This saw Dr James Mwangi come in as a turnaround manager.

There was high demand for banking services, and most banks had business models that were not very friendly to customers at the bottom of the pyramid. To stay afloat, Equity Building Society changed its business model to a microfinance services model, where short-term savings were matched with short-term loans.

As part of the turnaround strategy, Dr Mwangi prioritised making banking accessible and affordable by removing the requirement for a minimum deposit, account opening deposit, and charging a monthly ledger fee, which was a disincentive to keep money in a bank as it depleted customers' savings.

The bank also made it easy to open an account by removing the requirement for a passport-size photo since it took rural folks up to three weeks to get them processed at the nearest town. This meant that you had to make several trips to town before you could open an account.

Equity sought to demystify banking, which was at that time considered a preserve of the moneyed. No wonder at the time Equity started its turnaround in 1994, only four per cent of the bankable population had bank accounts. This percentage has over the years grown to over 87 per cent.

Because of its mass banking model, unlike other banks, Equity's banking halls were made with generous space, with an average branch measuring 8,000 – 10,000 square feet to accommodate as many customers as possible. To put this in perspective, the average banking hall for a corporate bank branch would measure about 2800-3000 square feet.

Due to the high demand for services, the branches became congested immediately after they were opened. This meant that the bank had to figure out a way of decongesting its banking halls.

After successfully piloting agency banking under the Social Payment Hunger Safety Net programme, where Equity distributed social stipends to beneficiaries in Northern Kenya through cash pay outs using points of sale managed by agents, the management saw no reason why it could not be used for commercial banking services. Equity was the first bank in the region to offer its services through the agency model. The model works by appointing the ordinary shopkeeper down the street and allowing them to take deposits and pay cash from a customer's account through a point of sale or a phone. The agent receives physical money from the customer and digitally credits the customer's account with a similar amount. The cash deposited by this customer is later used to pay a customer who would like to withdraw from their account by sending the agent the equivalent in digital money and receiving the corresponding amount in cash from the agent.

It had been proven that the risks in the model were extremely low. And after much back and forth with the Central Bank of Kenya, which did not at first believe that banking services could be offered outside a physical branch, the regulator finally approved agency banking in 2010. The beauty of this model is that all the costs are variable since the agent is paid based on the actual number of transactions processed.

The innovation was swiftly duplicated by all other banks in Kenya and the region. By this time, Equity had invested in a state-of-the-art core banking system named Finacle and a data centre that gave the bank the ability to run multiple banking channels, including branches, agencies, ATMs, and mobile banking that was first introduced around 2008.

When a customer opened an account, they would automatically be given an ATM card to allow them to withdraw cash and pay for goods and services at various outlets. When the cards first hit the market, one customer from Machakos town took matters too far in making sure his card would not be damaged by the elements.

He did not realise the downside of his rather comical action until he tried to make a withdrawal, and the card was rejected. After several unsuccessful attempts, he stormed into the banking hall, demanding to see the branch manager. The manager calmly asked him what the problem was. He fished his card out of his pocket and explained that the card that had been issued just a few minutes ago was not working. The manager could not hide his amusement when upon examining the card he realised that it had been laminated hence the malfunction!

The experience, as comical as it was, provided an invaluable lesson to the bank on the need to improve financial literacy and accessibility to its customers across all social classes.

—•••—

One of my first responsibilities, when I joined Equity, was to set up a legal department in the bank, which I successfully did. But I soon realised that if I stuck to my legal knowledge alone, I would not go very far in my new career path.

Banking is about people, relationships and growing the business. It is, therefore, important for the legal department to play a supportive role and not curtail the business. So, I set out to understand the values that drive the banking and financial services sector. I was also keen to come to grips with the bank's strategy as well as what the competition was up to.

To effectively play my role, I had to familiarise myself with such new terms as Return on Equity (ROE), Return on Assets (ROA), Non-performing Loans (NPLs) and cost-income ratios, seeing I did not have a finance background at the time. I also proactively studied the bank's financial statements to understand what each ratio meant to the business.

My efforts paid off, and I was promoted to the role of Company Secretary and later Director of Strategy also in charge of investor relations. The latter role helped me understand the mind of the investor and what was most important and of concern to them. Interactions with investors also widened my understanding of the business as they kept me on my toes with their feedback, sometimes in the form of harsh criticism of the bank.

I have had different experiences in each of the countries that the bank has expanded to. In Uganda, for instance, we started on the wrong footing, with the subsidiary making losses to the tune of $10 million (KSh1.2 billion) in the second year of acquisition on the back of poor internal controls and brand image management.

After a deep dive into what went wrong at the acquisition stage, we realised that we had adopted a flawed approach to governance, and we had to bite the bullet and make the necessary changes. We changed the management team and overhauled the board as well as key policies and procedures.

By the fifth year, the unit started showing signs of recovery under the able leadership of Samuel Kirubi who had grown to the role of subsidiary MD from an intern under the Equity Leadership Program(ELP) in 1998. There was also a marked improvement in our relationship with the regulator due to high compliance levels.

The positive thing about the several critical mistakes we had made in Uganda was that we learnt from them, and when we got an opportunity to acquire the Procredit Bank in 2015, we adopted a very different approach.

By the time of the acquisition, the bank had a balance sheet of only $150 million. But by 2020, when we wrapped up our second acquisition of Banque Commerciale Du Congo (BCDC), the Equity Bank Congo unit's balance sheet had grown to about $900 million, a more than seven-fold growth at a time when the country was going through a political transition.

The Democratic Republic of Congo (DRC) as a market, in our assessment, has very high potential with a banked population of only four per cent. We are convinced that with our business model that focuses on financial inclusivity and empowerment, we can significantly tap into the unbanked population of over 100 million people, creating more value for our shareholders.

Before the acquisition, BCDC was the second-largest in the market with an asset size of over $1.3 billion. On completion of the acquisition and merger in 2020, the combined balance sheet of the new entity Equity Banque Commerciale Du Congo (EBCDC) rose to over $3 billion, propelling Equity Group to become the largest lender in the region.

Serving on the Equity Board, initially as the Secretary to the Board, then as Company Secretary, and currently as the Group Executive Director has been an exciting and insightful journey for me.

As Secretary to the Board, I was responsible for keeping all the company records, including minutes, and also acting as an advisor to the Board on a range of issues, from legal compliance to risk management. This made the Chairman of the Board nickname me "our protector." Over time, I have learnt that doing the right things in the right way will always earn you the respect of both your juniors and seniors.

Juggling different roles at the same time has helped me get a good grasp of the bank's strategy, adequately preparing me for more responsibilities, including that of the Director of Corporate Strategy, which I held for several years.

Initially, it was not easy, but I have learnt to get out of my comfort zone and increase my knowledge of the business. I experienced my baptism by fire when I single-handedly had to face a team of investors after the Director of Credit got an emergency a few minutes before their meeting. He usually handled all the credit-related questions, but in his absence, I had to step in.

The investors included a team of young Harvard-trained analysts, who were asking all sorts of questions. Out of the blue, one of them asked me: "Mary, what is the cost of risk of Equity?"

My mind suddenly went blank. I was familiar with terms like non-performing loans and asset quality, but I had never heard of "the cost of risk." Before I could process the question, he added: "How do we calculate this ratio?" I was truly out of my depth.

Never one to shy away from a challenge, I composed myself. There is no way I was going to let a bunch of young analysts embarrass me.

"Thanks for the question. Now, if you look at the numbers, Equity does more loans in the microfinance sector. This means we give out small unsecured loans but in huge volumes. Yet, we have attained one of the best NPLs in the market at around 2.5 per cent.

We have the trust of our customers, and we trust them. Our customers would rather sell cows to pay their loans than to go into default because they have nowhere else to go…," I answered, growing confident by the moment.

The discussion continued. The analyst did not ask any follow-up questions, and I was off the hook.

After the meeting, I ran into Elizabeth Gathai, the then General Manager of Credit and now Group Director in charge of the Small and Medium Enterprise Sector.

I asked her: "Elizabeth, what is the cost of risk, and how do you calculate it?"

"Mary, you know this one. It is written off loans as a percentage of gross loans," she answered, smiling broadly at my ignorance. Of course, I knew that!

One of the greatest milestones during my time at Equity has been listing on the Nairobi Securities Exchange (NSE). Unknown to many, the move towards listing started in 2005 after the successful conversion of Equity Building Society to Equity Bank Limited as a full-fledged commercial bank.

When the two investment banks that served as the transaction advisors did a valuation to determine the listing price, they returned a value per share of Ksh70. Looking at the growth potential, we disputed the valuation as too low and not representative of the real value of Equity at the time.

When the investment banks insisted that this was the best valuation, the Board made an uncharacteristic decision to list on the Stock Exchange by an introduction (the first in the market), which meant coming to the stock market without offering any shares for sale to the public, only listing the existing shares.

Since it was the first time any Kenyan company had done this, the regulator was suspicious of the bank's true intentions. Were the shareholders looking for a quick way to dump their shares into the market? It took a long time to convince the regulator of the genuineness of the listing, and we finally struck a compromise by agreeing that all the major shareholders would be barred from selling their shares for two years after listing.

In the run-up to the listing, there were interesting discussions on the merit and demerits of the process. One school of thought was that it was like a man surrendering his he-goat, the most prized possession for a Kikuyu elder. The counter opinion was that it was better to be a small fish in a big ocean than a big fish in a pond.

The second opinion carried the day. The initial investors of Equity, although they have since been diluted, experienced unprecedented growth in the valuation of their investment. Eventually, on August 6, 2006, Equity Chairman Dr Peter Munga rang the bell to signal the commencement of trading of the bank's shares on the securities exchange.

There was a lot of excitement in the market, with the counter opening at a price of Ksh123 per share compared to the value of Ksh70 that the transaction advisors had quoted. This was a massive coup for Equity, signalling a new phase of growth for the bank into becoming the biggest bank in the country and the region. There was no turning back. The shareholders have since witnessed exponential value growth, spawning new millionaires and billionaires in the process.

In preparation for listing on the Nairobi bourse, where high levels of disclosure and transparency are demanded, we looked at the history of failed banks and credit institutions and the reasons why they failed. These were summarised in an analysis carried out by the regulator, the Central Bank of Kenya. One of the recurring themes in the failed lenders was failing to observe strict governance standards.

This was evidenced by directors borrowing from the institutions either directly or through their associates and not paying them back. Others traded with the institutions, creating a conflict of interest.

The first thing we had to do was to put checks and balances to ensure that this never happened in Equity. We passed a policy that board members could not borrow from the bank or trade with it. This policy helped the bank stand very firm from a governance perspective to date.

These policies are over and above other Central Bank-issued guidelines on governance. It has helped us ensure that we stay true to our mantra of "transforming lives, giving dignity, and expanding opportunities for wealth creation."

For an institution that had been declared technically insolvent in 1993, the turnaround is nothing short of spectacular. Equity is now East Africa's biggest bank with more than 400 branches, 18 million customers, and an asset base of over Ksh1.5 trillion ($ 15 billion) as of 30th March 2023, courtesy of its business model anchored on access, convenience, flexibility, and affordability.

Equity has over the years earned local and global accolades having been declared the best bank in Kenya by Think Business for over 10 years in a row besides being the subject of study in many global business schools, including Harvard, Stanford, Yale, MIT, Columbia, and Lagos, among others.

But when you start showing signs of success, especially when coming from an underdog position, it is only natural that you will attract enemies and friends in equal measure. We experienced this first hand between 2005 and 2008 when the bank's visibility increased.

During this time, there was a lot of adverse publicity, with some claiming that Equity was a bubble waiting to burst and that it was cooking its books. Those who did not understand the bank's business model and the concept of low margin, high volume concept wondered how a bank could make money from banking those at the bottom of the pyramid.

"They have no money to give you... and those loans will never be repaid. Wait, you will see how their non-performing loans will grow," some of our detractors sneered.

Contrary to expectations, the bank was growing on all fronts annually, and in 2006, we celebrated our one-millionth customer! By this time, the bank was registering a more than 100 per cent growth in profitability and exponential growth in loans and deposits.

The negative rumours in the market resulted in a Central Bank forensic audit conducted by KPMG, the renowned audit firm. However, no major irregularities were noted since there were none to begin with. The biggest lesson from this vicious onslaught by our detractors, and as our Group CEO James kept on reminding us, was to always remain clean so that if mud is thrown at you, it will not stick.

Because of the massive growth, the bank started struggling with capitalisation in 2007. After a competitive search for a suitable investor, Helios got the nod to acquire a 25 per cent stake in the bank in the biggest Foreign Direct Investment transaction in sub-Sahara Africa at the time valued at $185 million.

This gave the bank the muscle to start the regional expansion. I spearheaded the bank's entry into Uganda through a merger and acquisition deal with Uganda Microfinance Limited in 2008 as well as greenfield entries into South Sudan the following year.

I also oversaw our greenfield entry into Rwanda in 2011 and Tanzania in 2012. Later in 2015, another merger and acquisition deal saw Equity take over Procredit Bank followed by BCDC Bank in 2020 for a staggering $100 million. This has propelled Equity to become the largest and the most profitable bank in the region.

One of the things that has helped in my career progression has been taking professional courses. These include such areas as risk management, governance and strategy, leadership, and pension fund management, among others.

In 2014, I joined St John York University in the UK for a Master's degree in Leadership, Innovation and Change, which gave me a different perspective on how to deal with people at various levels. I also undertook the Advanced Management Programme at Harvard Business School in 2018.

THE ART OF BALANCE

04

"In all aspects of our lives, balance is key. Doing one thing too much can cause upset like the old saying goes, everything in moderation is the secret!"

— Catherine Pulsifer

Bringing up children as a career woman is no small feat. You must contend with many challenges, including dealing with pesky house girls - a working woman's worst nightmare.

There are days when you wake up and get ready for work, only for them to approach you as you are about to leave and quip: "Ma'am, I am going… I no longer want to work here." You are suddenly thrown into a spin, not knowing what to do about your court appearance to defend an accused person or a pre-planned meeting with an important client meant to start in two hours.

It is all part of the motherhood journey, which I immensely enjoyed. When I gave birth to our daughters Joy and Jacqueline, I was still in private legal practice. My days mainly revolved around meetings with clients and attending court sessions in Nairobi and out of town. Despite my busy work schedule, I still had to return to the house on time to attend to the children.

Using public transport to work and back home was not very reliable or efficient. But everyone raised in a modest background in the country had to start there. Though I started working in 1991, I bought my first car eight years later. It was a green Toyota Starlet, registration KAM 149C. I loved that car. I drove it until 2005, when I upgraded to a Toyota Harrier after joining Equity Bank the previous year.

Some days, I would leave the house as early as 4 am and drive from Nairobi to Meru, some 236km away, and be seated in court by 8.30 am, long before my counterpart from the locality arrived. On other days it would be an appearance for a client in the Nanyuki or Nakuru law courts, located in the present-day Laikipia and Nakuru Counties, respectively.

Despite my many travels, I rarely spent the night away from my family. The only work engagement that saw me spend the night away was in Kisii town, where I had to represent a client. I had not yet bought the Starlet, so I had to take public transport on a rickety bus christened "Abunwasi." Its top speed was about 50 kilometres per hour, so you can imagine how many hours it took to cover the distance of about 345km to Kisii. The bus would pull up at every stop and then passengers took their time buying samosas, bananas, drinks, and other foodstuffs from the mobile vendors.

Another time I travelled to Embu to attend a hearing at the Lands Registry. The matter was concluded at around 3 pm, and I rushed to the bus stop to catch a bus back to Nairobi. By 6.30 pm, it still had not filled up. When it became apparent there might not be enough passengers to make the journey, I alighted and enquired about alternative means to get back to the city. Some touts at the bus stage told me to try my luck on one of the buses that pass through the town from Meru.

By then, dusk was starting to set in. I had resigned to my fate of having to spend the night in the town and travel back the following morning. It was a tough choice as I could not imagine being away the entire night from my children, especially Jacqueline, who was two years old at the time.

Just as I was about to give up, I was directed to a Nissan van that ferried *Miraa* (khat) to Nairobi. The drivers of the vehicles are notorious for driving at break-neck speeds, and I was not sure if I wanted to risk my life riding on one. But the thought of being away from my babies tormented me even more. So, I decided to take the risk when they told me they had space for two passengers.

I said a short prayer as I squeezed myself into the van, and off we went. Long story short, 45 minutes later, we were offloading our cargo at California Estate in Nairobi, the first stop before the crew dropped me off 10 minutes later at the Kencom House Bus Stop.

I said a prayer of thanksgiving to God for delivering me back safely and went home to my children, who were eagerly waiting for me.

This experience highlights the plight of career women who juggle family roles as part of civic duties. Like many other working mothers, at times, I would wonder if I was giving enough time to my children or if I was sacrificing them at the altar of career progression.

We had a lot of fun when the children were young. We had many family trips within Nairobi and far-flung places like Mombasa and Malindi. We still go on family trips together, a routine that started when the children were younger to unwind and bond.

I also had my fair share of embarrassing moments as a mother. When Joy was about four years old, and Jacqueline was still a nursing infant, we went for the air-show at Nairobi's Wilson Airport. As we enjoyed watching the planes zoom by, Joy wandered off and disappeared into the thick crowd.

Every parent's worst nightmare of losing their child was unravelling right before my eyes. I was beside myself with worry and started crying after failing to trace her in the milling crowd. After a long futile search, we decided to go to the lost children's corner, and there was Joy happily nibbling at some biscuits and sipping soda without a care in the world!

Another time we went for a trip to the Coast with my friends Josephine Sichangi, Felistus Njoroge, Veronica Mbugua, Mukami Muthee and Julia Kariuki with our families. We had planned to go to Malindi and hired three vehicles for the trip. We stopped at a hotel for refreshments and thereafter we each got into our respective vehicles and drove off. I did not realise we had left Joy (again!) behind after she delayed in the washroom.

She came out just as we disappeared down the road, and she frantically tried waving at us, but no one noticed her. By God's grace, a patron who was pulling up into the hotel noticed the whole drama and offered to give chase in his car along with Joy. I was so embarrassed and terrified at the same time about what could have happened had that good Samaritan not been there. Up to today, Joy still asks me: "How could you forget your own child?"

Jacqueline, on the other hand, when young, was the mischievous type. One time during mass at the Holy Family Cathedral in Nairobi, she ran to the altar after all the offertory bags had been returned and fished out a handful of cash and brought it back to me.

"Mum, this is for you," she said, innocently handing me the cash.

I was left at a loss whether to return the money or keep it amid accusing looks from the rest of the congregation.

Her mischievous side came to the fore again during a visit to the Maasai Ostrich Farm in Kitengela on the outskirts of Nairobi, East Africa's largest commercial hub for ostrich farming. It was a warm Sunday afternoon, and the children were having the time of their life in the swimming pool.

I sat at a distance watching the children as I sipped a cold drink, when suddenly, there was an unusual commotion in the parking area. A convoy of vehicles had just pulled up, and a team of suited gentlemen waving walkie-talkies had rushed in to control the milling crowd.

As soon as the black limousine bedecked in a small flag (the President's standard) at the front came to a stop, one of the menacing-looking men rushed to the back door and held it open.

Finally, the VIP stepped out, holding his trademark *rungu* (traditional baton) and waved to the crowd before being led to a table at one end of the compound. It was the late former President of the Republic of Kenya, Daniel Arap Moi.

No sooner had the President and his entourage settled than Jacqueline, who had noticed the commotion jumped out of the pool and, before anyone could restrain her ran to the VIP table. I could only watch with my mouth wide open as President Moi's security detail tried to stop her. He noticed the scuffle and waved them away, beckoning Jacqueline to come forward.

"Hello, Baba Moi," she quipped, stretching out her hand to greet the late President. They had a brief conversation before she trotted back to our table, smiling ear to ear and triumphantly declaring: "I have greeted Baba Moi."

I didn't know whether to reprimand her or congratulate her for her boldness as she ran back to the pool. That was Jacqueline for you.

Nine years after Jacqueline was born, we welcomed our third born, Lisa, our little drama queen. During a family vacation to Seychelles, when she was about two, she threw a huge tantrum on the plane.

"Open the door, I want to come out!" she kept shouting, much to the amusement of the other passengers.

When we got to the hotel, her bad mood continued as she ran around the lobby, breaking all the ashtrays before we could restrain her. Her mood, however, brightened after check-in, and we enjoyed our stay on the enchanting island.

Seeing the children grow through the different life stages was a joy. Today, they are all grown, with Joy having completed a Masters of Business Administration study at Rotman Business School in Toronto, Canada. Jacqueline, on the other hand, is a career woman in creative advertising, having graduated with a Degree in Business Management from the University of Sussex, while Lisa is about to join the university soon.

Getting married into the Maranga family was a real blessing. I particularly had a good relationship with my father-in-law, the late David Maranga. Having grown up without a father figure, Mr Maranga became the father I never had. He doted on his grandchildren and would gladly drive us to the village in Nyeri in his pick-up for the children to visit their grandmother.

Mr Maranga operated a bar in Nairobi and would religiously travel home to Nyeri every weekend to see my mother-in-law Margaret Maranga and the rest of the family. The children and I enjoyed riding in his pick-up to Mathira. We would stop at his favourite butchery in Makutano to pick up some meat.

Until his death in 2018, we remained close. I miss his fatherly advice.

During our many trips to the village, I also enjoyed catching up with my sister-in-law Jacinta Wambura and other relatives who would come to say hello. One of the most profound moments in my life was the untimely loss of Jacinta, who was the eldest in her family.

On that fateful day in 2009, the entire extended family had gathered at our house in Lavington Nairobi for New Year celebrations. Before the stroke of midnight, we shared communion and a hearty meal. As the night progressed amid the merry-making, I noticed Jacinta was unusually quiet. When I enquired if she was okay, she disclosed that she had been diagnosed with a heart ailment and was feeling very tired. She was under treatment which I believed was working well. The bad news shook me to the core. Despite her ill health, she had hitherto remained stoic and bubbly as ever.

After the New Year celebrations, Jacinta's health deteriorated, and on 4th January 2010 she collapsed in her residence and was pronounced dead on arrival at the Nairobi Hospital.

Her death hit me in a way I had not expected, leaving a big void that I have not been able to fill up to now. It made me appreciate the fragility of life and appreciated those closest to me even more, particularly my mother. Her beautiful daughter Eleanor Wangui will hopefully carry on with her legacy. Together with her two children Jayden and Imani they will collectively continue carrying Jacinta's torch and keep it shining bright.

Two years prior to Jacinta's passing, my Mum had started ailing. One Sunday morning as we returned from a Mount Kenya road trip, my husband Wamae and I decided to pass by her home in Tetu. As we drove into the compound, we noticed that it was unusually quiet. On a typical Sunday, my Mum would have been up early to attend mass at her local church before returning home for lunch.

We were disturbed to learn that she was still in bed and had missed mass earlier in the day. This was very unusual, and I knew that something was wrong. She said she was feeling unwell, but it was nothing serious. She managed to get up from her bed and chatted with us during our short stay. However, as we were about to leave, I noticed she was sweating profusely.

I suggested to Wamae we bring her to Nairobi to see a doctor the following day. To our dismay, she was diagnosed with both diabetes and hypertension and was immediately put on treatment. From then on, she would periodically come to Nairobi for review and to pick up her prescription drugs.

In 2011, her health took a turn for the worse and was admitted to the Nairobi Hospital for several days. At this point, I realised that she was not capable of taking care of herself at home back in the village and asked her to move in with us so that we could take care of her. She reluctantly agreed. She stayed with us until 2017 when she suffered a heart attack and passed on while undergoing treatment in the ICU on June 21st.

Even in her final moments, she insisted on praying for everyone who had gathered at her bedside, including my cousin John Baptista Gichuhi, a Catholic priest, who administered the final rites to her.

When she was taken ill a week earlier, and admitted to hospital I was on a business trip to the United States and had to cut it short to be by her bedside. She was not able to say much in her final days, but I still remember what would be her parting shot to me: "Wangari be careful in life, and always be alert because there are many detractors out there who do not mean well." One of the valuable lessons I learnt from her was to never complain despite the difficult circumstances we may find ourselves in at times.

Despite her failing health, she kept a good attitude of gratitude and would always quip whenever someone asked her how she was doing: "We thank God for everything." She also never missed saying her rosary daily and reciting prayers from the "Pieta" prayer book besides occasionally attending mass at our local church. As it became more difficult for her to move around, we would organise for a priest to administer Holy Communion at home.

She never missed an opportunity to remind my children and I about the importance of putting God first in everything. I truly miss her and whenever I need divine guidance, I call upon her angels to intercede for me and my family in keeping with my Catholic faith.

Time is a key commodity and a success factor in life, but it's never enough. One of the important things I have learnt over the years as I have grown in my career is that managing my time is key to obtaining a healthy work-life balance.

You achieve this by getting your priorities right in terms of the time you spend at work and with your family. It calls for sacrifices, including sometimes giving up outings with social peers (girlfriends) to put in a few hours at work or be with my family.

I discovered early on that some of the stressful moments we have in life are because we want to be "supermen/women" who can do all. I accepted that I could not make dinner for my family daily and so had to enlist the help of a house-help. When the children were young, I could not pick them up from school daily and had to contract a driver to do so sometimes.

Despite my busy schedule, I always cook for my family on Sundays (to date), and give my house-help the day off. I especially love cooking and enjoying a special vegetable soup that my late Mum loved so much too.

When my children were younger, I always made sure I attended their school events and meetings unless I was travelling. I particularly miss attending sports events at Riara School, where Lisa attended kindergarten and her primary school education.

Lisa joined Riara School in Kindergarten and she loved the school so much, I really miss the sports days and other events when the Director Dr Edda Gachukia would address us parents and the children we all would loudly respond in unison to her greeting "Good Morning Cucu (grandmother)!"

The children are bigger now, but to maintain a sense of community, we still go on trips and holidays together to relax and bond, especially during the school holidays when they are at home.

I cannot forget this one time my children sprung a real surprise on me. They conspired and in deep secrecy executed their plot in a manner that I had previously not thought them capable of doing. I celebrated my 50th birthday on 7th July 2018. I planned that we would have the same usual cake at home plus dinner. I had an early School Board meeting in Nyeri and I planned to come back home in time for the birthday cake. Then my friend Jemimah Kiarie called me and told me she wanted to buy me dinner and that she had something very serious and urgent to discuss. Jemimah is not the friend that calls you for nothing so I confirmed. Just before I left for dinner, I noticed that the house was unusually deserted and so I called my girls to ask where they were and gave a different story but since it was a Saturday, I didn't think much of it.

So, I met Jemimah at Java Karen Crossroads and she suggested we go have a decent meal at Dari Restaurant in Karen presently Tamambo. We drove in and she said she had reserved a particular room to which we proceeded. The room was in darkness and I was just telling her it seemed that Kenya Power had decided we would have a blackout when the lights suddenly went on. What I saw surprised me pleasantly. The room was full of my siblings, cousins, close friends and colleagues. Unknown to me they had arranged a birthday party and I had no inkling of what was happening at all. I later learnt that they all had been sworn to utmost confidentiality including my cousin Fr JB Gichuhi, Beatrice Kamau the decor provider who is also a close friend, my siblings etc and none mentioned the secret to me. It was so special and I will never forget it. As I grow older, I have come to appreciate simple gestures like this one done in love.

Every day I say a prayer of thanksgiving and gratitude to God for the special gift of my children. I pray for them daily that the Lord may guide and lead them to paths of great fulfilment and success.

—••••—

EARNING A SEAT IN THE BOARDROOM

05

*"I didn't learn to be quiet when I had an opinion.
The reason they knew who I was is because I told
them."*

— Ursula Burns

When I joined Equity Building Society in 2004, the Board membership was male-dominated.

Following the transition into a commercial bank later in the year, we needed to dissolve the old Board and transfer the assets and liabilities of the Building Society to the new entity, which was a limited liability company incorporated in December 2004 following licensing by the Central Bank of Kenya.

It was necessary to reconstitute the Board to accommodate a new reality. One of the critical considerations for the reconstitution of the Board was that it needed to take into account the principle of diversity based on gender, age, skills and regional balance.

We achieved some level of diversity, and for the first time, two women gained seats on the Board. And to give it the face of Kenya, the bank brought in directors from the Coast, Nyanza, Western, Rift Valley and

Central Kenya. There was also a deliberate effort over the years to infuse young blood into the Board, who would bring in new ideas.

One of my biggest roles during Equity's high growth phase was to make sure that the bank's relationship with various stakeholders was well managed. Being a listed company, it calls for high levels of disclosure and transparency.

As the Company Secretary, a role I served in between 2005 and 2018, I was charged with ensuring that the Board carried out its oversight function effectively without interfering with the management. I also oversaw the establishment of board committees to support the Board to fulfil its mandate as provided for by regulatory guidelines.

There are six board committees, namely the Audit, Risk and ALCO, Sustainability, Strategy and Investments, IT, Innovations & Cyber Security and Governance & Nominations committees to take care of the emerging needs of the business and support the execution of the broader strategy of the Equity Group. Equity Group Holdings Plc, the listed holding company Board currently has four women, which is about 50 per cent of the board. The Vice-Chairperson is a woman Mrs Evelyn Rutagwenda, a Rwandese citizen. This is a big achievement considering where we have come from. We are working deliberately to increase women representation.

As Company Secretary, I had to keep abreast of the principles of good corporate governance. Good stakeholder management is at the core of effectively building social capital. Maintaining a good relationship with the various stakeholders enables Equity Group to tailor its strategy to meet their needs. It was important for me to ensure that the engagement with stakeholders was defined by the core values of the Group that are captured under the acronym P-I-C-T-U-R-E, standing for Professionalism, Integrity, Creativity and Innovation, Teamwork, Unity of Purpose, Respect and Dignity for customers, and Effective Corporate Governance.

Shareholders are concerned with efficient capital allocation, sustainable growth and high returns. Other considerations include sustainability in business practices, a strong management team and transparency and disclosure. This has been achieved by convening annual general meetings and regular investor briefings per the Group's listing obligations.

The bank is obliged to comply with all legal and regulatory requirements, pay all the taxes due promptly and actively participate in industry working groups on top of embracing good corporate governance. During my tenure as Company Secretary, I ensured that the policies and procedures of the bank were updated regularly to capture the dynamism of the market and timely submission of all necessary reports and returns.

I also oversaw relevant partnerships on education, health, and resource conservation. Several Development Financial Institutions, such as the International Finance Corporation, European Investment Bank, KfW of Germany, The MasterCard Foundation, and African Development Bank entered into an arrangement with the bank to extend support in the form of technical support, risk sharing guarantees, financial literacy training, entrepreneurship training and other capacity building programs in small and medium enterprises, agriculture, clean energy initiatives primarily to support youth and women.

As Company Secretary, I spearheaded several initiatives that have resulted in an elaborate and scalable governance framework that provides transparency and controls in delivering value to the business. To do this, I dedicated a significant amount of time to studying various governance principles.

My role included advising the Board on compliance with various statutes, including convening all statutory meetings as well as Annual General Meetings. I also provided secretarial services to the Board.

Gaining and taking up a seat on the Board as a woman was challenging but also insightful. I imbibed as much knowledge as possible on the Group's strategy and risk management approaches during Board meetings. I was privileged to participate in key meetings, including those where decisions on expansion into new markets in the region such as Uganda, South Sudan, Tanzania, Rwanda, and the Democratic Republic of Congo were taken. This made me appreciate different cultures and practices as well as opportunities and threats in each market.

Having watched and reviewed many Boards of peer organisations over the years, I not only noticed the underrepresentation but also developed a keen interest in advocating for more women on corporate boards. The workplace is, however, tough for women who have to juggle careers, family, and other societal pressures and prejudices.

For women, therefore, to rise through the corporate ladder and occupy the C-suite of any organisation in a male-dominated space takes both deliberate short and long-term planning. You have to stand out in your line of work to earn the respect of your male colleagues.

I attribute my success in the corporate world to passion and finding a purpose in my job on top of putting in the hours. Some attribute their success to working smart and not hard. I say you have to work both smart and hard at the same time to realise lasting and enviable success. There is no substitute for hard work!

The danger of being too ambitious and a go-getter as a woman is that you may be perceived as rude and aggressive. If you are too nice, you become a pushover for everyone. And, you have to walk a tightrope, in keeping with public opinion.

When it comes to getting things done, I have learnt to be nice and respectful but assertive in a way that does not compromise my core beliefs and values. I always make sure I'm armed with the relevant information to defend my position. This modus operandi has earned me the nickname the "Iron Lady" in some quarters.

In the boardroom, I learnt the basic principles of communication, always being diplomatic even if I disagreed with someone's position and backing my argument with the necessary facts.

Time is a valuable but limited resource for everyone with multiple tasks to undertake. I have a full plate all the time. Despite my busy schedule, I have had to strike a balance between my work and family time.

I have also come to appreciate that there will always be fundamental differences in how men and women view things, but this should not necessarily create conflict as it can be used to broaden our perspectives. All that both genders need are the right opportunities and tools to compete on a level playing field. As a woman, you need to develop a thick skin to withstand the gender bias that sometimes may lock you out of certain opportunities.

In 2018, after serving in the Corporate Secretary role for 13 years, I was appointed the Group Executive Director, giving me a seat on all the boards of the Group's subsidiaries. Giving up the Corporate Secretary's position was not easy. If you are in the same role for that long and you enjoy what you are doing it is natural to hold on and doubt if someone else can do it as well, but I have realised that for you to continue to grow in your profession or career you must accept to keep reinventing yourself and taking on different challenges.

The role was actually split into 3: Company Secretary with Lydia Ndirangu now serving in that role supported by Stephen Muendo, Chief Strategy Officer and Investor relations with Brent Malahay currently serving in that role and Legal Services which is now an independent division headed by Gertrude Wamala. Even for entrepreneurs, especially sole founders of family businesses, there must come a time to yield to others to lead and to take positions under our leadership and bring fresh knowledge, new perspectives and energy into the business.

Sitting on the Boards of Equity Group's 11 subsidiaries has come with its fair share of challenges and opportunities. In my new capacity, I act as the link between the board and the Executive Management and the subsidiaries' management teams and the Group Corporate Office to ensure that the teams receive the necessary support to execute their mandate.

This role requires that I attend all quarterly Board meetings in our six countries of operation in the region, including Kenya, every quarter. It is such a hectic schedule because of regulatory requirements for the publication of financial results so all meetings have to be concluded within four weeks of start to allow for consolidation of Group results. By the end of each Board season, I would have attended about 60 committees and full board meetings, but I was taught the value of hard work and I do what I have to do. My mentor Dr James Mwangi always reminds me that things don't just happen. They are made to happen through seamless and speedy execution of strategy.

My motto is "no pain no gain" and so I gladly embrace the challenges that come with the role.

I appreciate the faith shown by my co-Directors to resolve any issues raised by the boards in respective countries. One of my greatest responsibilities as Group Executive Director is to ensure that the subsidiaries seamlessly replicate Equity's business model across the region, albeit with some adjustments to meet the needs of their respective markets. As the business expands into new horizons the Board recently promoted the former Managing Director of our Uganda subsidiary, Samuel Kirubi, to the Group Chief Operations Officer; and together, we shall provide the necessary oversight.

In recognition of my role in the growth of the Equity Group in 2021, I was named the overall winner of the inaugural Angaza Awards in the "Women To Watch In Banking and Finance 2021" category. I led nine other winners in various categories who had been shortlisted for the top prize in the awards, which saw 40 entries from Kenya, Uganda, Tanzania, Rwanda and South Sudan.

Angaza Awards, recognise purpose-driven women leaders in banking and finance who show exemplary leadership and commitment to the industry. The winners were drawn from banking, microfinance, Saccos, capital markets, fin-techs, fund management and investment banking.

The judges focused on scale and impact. They not only wanted to know how contestants had contributed to the success of their organisations but also their professional achievements and impact on society, according to Catherine Musakali, one of the judges and co-founder of Women on Boards Network Kenya.

I was honoured to receive the overall award, with the judges citing the winner "as a woman steering and shaping the region's financial services sector." Young women need role models, and I hope that this award inspires them to take up the challenge of leadership in their respective areas.

In my acceptance speech, I committed to mentoring and coaching others. The awards were hosted by the Kenya Bankers Association, which is the leading advocacy group and umbrella body of licensed banks in the country.

Hot on the heels of the Angaza Awards, I was pleasantly surprised to be declared the overall winner of the "Woman on Board Awards 2021" organised by the Women on Boards Network. The awards celebrate individuals and organisations that have changed the landscape and who champion gender diversity in Corporate Boards. They recognise efforts that promote gender parity and equity in the social economic status of women and youth.

In this respect, I was awarded for the establishment of the Equity Inspire Programme (EQUIP) at the 2020 International Women's Day (IWD). The conception of the program was a direct result of the gaps that I personally experienced in terms of intentional support for women aspiring to leadership positions or board positions in most institutions. Most of the time the women have to grapple through a maze of complexity, rapidly changing environment and stiff competition to move to the next level. Concerted efforts to prepare women for leadership positions is hence necessary.

The IWD brings together women from all walks of life to share ideas on how to increase the participation of women in leadership, social-economic and other spheres of life. The EQUIP programme aims to ensure that the bank creates the right policies for women to compete with men for opportunities. It also encourages women to build their leadership skills and confidence to take on more challenging roles in the senior management of the bank.

The programme at the same time facilitates the networking of women to support their quest for better positions in the bank and elsewhere and drive the agenda for equality. As part of this programme, we organise talks, webinars and videos of successful women and male leaders in various disciplines to share lessons learnt and advise on what women should look out for as they build successful careers.

In 2021, a select group of women participated in the Women 4 Growth Programme courtesy of The Swedfund where they discussed issues like perceptions that limit growth, organisation facilitation that limits growth, mental health, motherhood and women's health, discrimination at the workplace, safe working environment and equal job opportunities, among other topics.

In 2021, the bank also established the EQUIP Book Club, starting with Robin Sharma's *A Leader Who Had No Title*. I am the patron of the book club. Some 1,553 ladies took part in reading and discussing the book, identifying lessons in groups of 10 over a six weeks period.

At the grand finale session, each group recounted their lessons to the entire group. Most of the members attested that reading the book impacted their lives positively both from a personal and professional/career perspective. We also do a survey and use the comments to improve the Club. Many testify how this program has inspired them to take on bigger challenges and confidently apply for new positions with confidence.

The book club's second book was *Lean In* by the former Chief Operations Officer at Facebook, in which she urges women to stand up for themselves at work and home. For Equip Book Club Cycle 3 we are reading the book "*The Psychology of Money*" by Morgan Housel which talks about money management and budgeting.

SUCCESS LESSONS FROM FAILURE AND ADVERSITY

CHAPTER 06

Do not judge me by my success, judge me by how many times I fell down and got back up again."

— Nelson Mandela

One morning in June 2017, my youngest brother, Edwin Kibaara, rang me up. Uncharacteristic of him, he sounded frantic. "Mum has been taken ill," he said.

It was a warm summer day in Washington DC, but I suddenly felt my entire body go cold.

"What do you suggest we should do? he asked as I steadied myself on a nearby chair.

Here I was, thousands of miles away in the capital of the world's most powerful nation, but powerless to do anything for my ailing Mum in her hour of need. The Group Chief Executive Officer had designated me to attend the official launch of Dana Redford's book, *Developing Africa's Financial Services: The Importance of High Impact Entrepreneurship.*

The book was based on a World Bank-sponsored Case Study on Equity Bank by David B Zoogah and Christian Wolf titled *"Equity Bank: From Humble Beginnings to Market Leader: A High Impact Entrepreneurial Turnaround Story."*

Coincidentally, I had been invited to attend a two-day event by Robin Sharma, my favourite inspirational writer, in Toronto Canada around the same time. And so, I thought: "Why not kill two birds with one stone?"

When I got the call, I had just arrived in Washington from Toronto through Montreal. In between the two events, I was to attend a dinner in honour of The Mastercard Foundation President, Ms Reeta Roy, after receiving an honorary degree from McGill University in Montreal for the foundation's work in the financial space.

The MasterCard Foundation had for more than 12 years been a great supporter of some of the Community social impact programmes under the Equity Group Foundation, including the Wings to Fly scholarship programme. Under this programme, more than 55,000 needy and disadvantaged children have so far benefited from the programme.

The Mastercard Foundation also supports Equity Bank's Young Africa Works programme that supports entrepreneurship by offering financial literacy and training to micro and small businesses. So far, more than 2.4 million women and youth as well as 400,000 businesses have benefited from the initiative under the financial literacy programme.

When I learnt about my Mum's illness, I had to cut short my trip abroad and got on the next available flight from Washington. On landing at the Jomo Kenyatta International Airport, I headed straight to The Nairobi Hospital, where my family had rushed her following my conversation with my brother. She was elated to see me upon arrival. I ensured she was comfortable before heading home.

The following day, I prepared Mum's favourite vegetable soup. This soup is made from green pepper, courgettes, onions, broccoli or mushroom or butternut, sweetly spiced up with a mix of parsley, basil, black pepper, coriander and others. She hated hospital food, and the soup was a welcome relief.

This, however, turned out to be her last meal. Later in the day, her condition worsened, and she was transferred to the Intensive Care Unit where she would be in a semi-coma for the next few days. Over the next few days when she was in the hospital, we hoped against hope that she would pull through as she had previously on the two occasions she was admitted.

➤ •●•●

On June 21, 2017, I sat at my desk blankly staring at the computer screen. However much I tried to concentrate on my work, my mind kept on wandering to my mum lying in the ICU. By 3 pm, I couldn't have it anymore. I shut down my computer, excused myself and drove to the Nairobi Hospital.

I was joined by other family members and a few friends. Being the pre-Covid-19 era, there were not many restrictions on visiting patients. We huddled in the waiting area, praying silently before a few of us were allowed to see her.

She had woken up from her coma just a few hours earlier, but you wouldn't tell as she insisted on leading prayers. The doctor came to see her later in the evening before gathering the family together for an update. His prognosis for her relapse was grim and startling.

"Her blood pressure is too low, and all efforts to stabilise it are not working. She is, therefore, likely to suffer another heart attack. We are, however, doing everything we can to make sure that does not happen," said Dr Kisyoka before leaving the room. This was one of the most devastating news I have ever received in my life.

I left the hospital at around 7.30 pm after making sure she was comfortable. Thirty minutes later just as I was stepping into the house, the hospital called. "We need you to come back," said the caller without giving more details. "The doctor will brief you when you get here," she added before hanging up. Mum had suffered a heart attack in December 2016 but this had been arrested in good time.

As I drove back to the hospital, all kinds of emotions went through my mind. "Did she suffer another heart attack, is she okay?" I wondered as I battled traffic on Argwings Kodhek Road. When I burst into the lobby of the hospital's ICU ward, one of the nurses confirmed my fears that she had suffered another heart attack, and the medical team attending to her was in the process of trying to resuscitate her.

I quickly turned back, fearing the worst. From the doctor's earlier explanation, hospital procedures required resuscitation to be carried out for about 30 minutes.

If the patient would not come around, they are declared clinically dead. By the time I walked in, the procedure had been going on for the said time, and there was nothing more the doctors could do. I was finally allowed in to say my goodbyes. Her long struggle with ill health had come to an end; she was finally at peace. Standing there by her bedside watching her lifeless body, I was engulfed by untold grief.

Tears welled up in my eyes, and I did not hold back until someone tapped me on the back, telling me it was time to go. I reluctantly walked out of the room as one of the medical staff prepared to move her body to the morgue.

I had lost a mentor and role model. Her final years living with my family cemented our friendship. She was my adviser and a pillar of strength because of her never-failing faith in God, which kept me going when things got tough. The days following Mum's death passed in a haze. I was yet to come to terms with her death.

We finally laid her to rest on July 31, 2017 in Tetu on the land she had tilled to and raised us up. Sometimes I hear her voice in my head calling me: "Wangari!" and I find myself absentmindedly answering: "Yes Mum…"

In 2015 during one of our annual family get-togethers, I suggested to my siblings we immortalise Mum's incredible life of resilience in a book. At the time of her death, the book, titled *Corneliah Wanjiru My Journey: A Memoir of My Life, Family and Faith* was already done, and we were in the process of picking photos to accompany the text.

The book's launch was slated for August 2017, but following her untimely death, we pushed the launch forward to coincide with her burial, where we distributed several copies to family, friends and other mourners.

Recounting the story of her life always makes me feel one with her again.

"Pain comes from within and you are free to let go of pain"
– Marcus Aurelius

On the first day of admission to the University of Nairobi on June 15th, 1987, I was walking down the winding tunnel that connects the Main Campus to the halls of residence on the other side of Uhuru Highway when one of the young men in the throng of new students behind me caught up with me.

"Hi, my name is Patrick," he introduced himself. "I'm Mary," I answered, trying to balance the huge suitcase in my right hand and the rucksack on my left shoulder.

We struck up a conversation before parting ways at the exit of the tunnel. From our brief encounter, I learnt that his full name was Patrick Wamae Maranga and had just been admitted to the Faculty of Medicine. Thus began a friendship that would only blossom into a serious relationship upon my graduation in 1990.

I graduated two years ahead of him because his medical course takes six academic years as opposed to four for most other courses. We got engaged soon after and married according to Kikuyu customary law in 1992 while Patrick was still a student. We solemnised our marriage 13 years later in 2005 at Don Bosco Shrine of Mary Help of Christians Church in Upper Hill, Nairobi.

We were blessed with three beautiful children - Joy Wangui born in 1992, Jacqueline Wanjiru (1995), and Lisa Wambura (2004).

Our marriage ended in 2018 after two years of separation. The decision to end a marriage I had built over more than 25 years was not an easy one, but suffice it to say it had become irretrievably broken. Following the divorce, I had a hard time trying to understand how I could successfully execute many complex projects at my workplace so effortlessly, yet fail in the most important "personal project" - my marriage.

The post-divorce season was very difficult. There are many stakeholders in the marriage besides the other spouse that one has to deal with. The most important of them are the children, who are the most affected emotionally. Then there are the immediate family members and close friends, who see you as the perfect couple but have no idea about what happens behind closed doors.

When the marriage breaks down, these stakeholders tend to take sides, not fully realising the role the other party played in the ending of the union. One of the surprises I got from this experience was that I lost some close friends. On the converse, some friends with whom I had not taken time to build relationships came very strong for me and stood in the gap at a very critical moment. Talk of the silver lining in every cloud.

The Catholic Church, like any other Christian faith, has a "till-death-do-us-part" approach to marriage, which puts the faithful in an awkward position when it happens. For the first time in my life, I felt like my faith in God and belief in the doctrines of my Catholic Church had faltered. My wounds have since healed, and currently, I am working very hard to rebuild my faith and redefine my interaction with the church.

A shaky faith in myself was part of the conundrum I found myself in after the initial separation in 2016. I was in a state of numbness, where I could not process all the emotions. Initially, I suppressed the anger, pain, and bitterness; in a sense, I was not sure how I felt.

I finally sought the help of a therapist, who assured me that marriage is not as easy as carrying out a merger and acquisition deal in the Bank. The main difference is that in a merger, one has control of all the decisions required to move the deal forward. But in a marriage, it takes two to tango. Simply put, the success of the union depends on the actions and reactions of both parties.

This made me feel better and enabled me to regain control of my life. I started enjoying a feeling of gratitude for all the good things in my life such as my children, good health, a support system of family and friends, and a rewarding socially impactful job. In addition to this, I also had some very strong shoulders to lean on. Jemimah Wakini Kiarie and Rosa Nduati Mutero, friends for a long time together with my family, were at hand to make sure I stayed on the straight and narrow path and vetted my thoughts and decisions for any possible irrationality. Several other friends gave me words of encouragement on different aspects that I needed to deal with. We all need friends for life. Yes, people who will be there for you at the darkest hour, not just during the great harvest years. Friends who will tell you to your face when you are doing or about to do something stupid and act as your accountability partners. I am grateful that I have these categories of special friends.

Today, I am at peace with how my life turned out. I would not wish to be in somebody else's shoes. I strive to become a better version of myself every day and impact others positively in a way that when my time on earth is over, I will not have wasted my God-given talents.

A famous quote by Gautama Buddha sums up this painful phase of my life: *"Anger is the punishment we give ourselves for someone else's mistake."* We have to acknowledge our humanity and admit our vulnerability to truly get rid of the pain and anger within us. Only then are we able to get complete healing and give a helping hand to those, who like us, need help to cope with difficult circumstances.

I have also come to appreciate the words of the famous author Paulo Coelho of *The Alchemist,* among other books: *"If you are brave enough to say goodbye, life will reward you with a new hello."*

—•••—

Sometime in 2005, a high-powered delegation of Equity Bank landed at Heathrow Airport in London. The team was led by the founding Chairman Dr Peter Munga, the CEO Dr James Mwangi and other senior managers, including myself.

The trip was a culmination of months of research that showed that there was a huge Kenyan diaspora community in London that the bank could tap into by opening a branch there. In our assessment, it would not be as simple as opening a branch in Nairobi's Gikomba.

We had done our homework and identified a strategic location in an area called Barking in East London. After successfully negotiating a lease with the property agent, we had planned to hold a customer dinner to popularise the new branch as we worked on the regulatory approvals from the UK government.

We identified a young lady by the name of Washuka Njongeri to run the branch. She would help customers open accounts and offer headquarters the necessary support to run the branch from Nairobi.

We consulted someone who understood UK laws to ensure compliance before the full rollout of operations. Their assessment of the viability of our venture was jarring. For starters, UK laws, from labour requirements to taxation, were completely different from Kenya's; and, therefore, not easy to implement remotely from Nairobi.

The writing was on the wall: we needed to shelve the idea and think it through before rolling it out despite logistics for getting the office up and running already having kicked into gear.

We realised that to carry out the intended business, we needed to open an account with a UK bank, which we thought would be easy since the entire top management of Equity Bank was in London. The first two banks we walked into were digital, with all services online, and there was no one to answer our queries.

At the third bank, the first requirement was proof of residence. In the UK, you can only get a residence permit after six months, which qualifies you for a social security number. The latter is your identity. To begin with, none of us had a residence visa and because we had no intentions of staying anyway, we could not get a social security number. We sought legal advice and we were informed that there was no getting around this requirement.

During our trip, I went shopping for a safe box to keep cash and other valuables. Together with other items, the bill came to about £1,500. The cashier was alarmed when I fished out the crisp notes from my handbag.

"Where are you from?" she posed, hesitating to take the cash. "I am from Kenya, Nairobi to be exact," I answered, wondering whether this was another classic case of racial profiling, which is an all-too-common occurrence in the West. "Here no one carries that much cash," said the cashier. That is when I realised her reason for regarding me with suspicion.

Long story short, I paid for the safe box, and it was safely delivered to my office by the time we got back. It, however, turned out that it was way above the weight allowed by the building safety regulations of London! After spending all that money, I had another huge problem on my hands!

Finally, we decided to abandon the idea of a brick-and-mortar branch in London. Sometimes in life, you have to know when you have been defeated and learn from your mistakes.

My assessment of why the London branch failed is that we had not done sufficient due diligence to understand the legal requirements of such a huge undertaking. We took a lot for granted, assuming that UK authorities would be impressed by the opportunity for a top Kenyan bank to invest in their country. To borrow from a common Kenyan saying, "things on the ground couldn't have been more different."

After the debacle, we had to go back to the drawing board and think outside the box for a way to support our diaspora customers who had already opened accounts with us. As I sat on the Kenya Airways Flight back to Nairobi from Heathrow, I remembered the quote by Sir Winston Churchill: "Success consists of going from failure to failure without loss of enthusiasm."

Lessons learnt from the failure of the London venture became the foundation for the current International Banking and Payments branch. The branch now has a dedicated team, which though domiciled in Nairobi's Kilimani, can serve customers in different time zones all over the world 24/7.

The branch has so far mobilised over Ksh4 billion in deposits and issued loans of about Ksh 2.5 billion to our customers in the diaspora besides assisting them process billions in payments and investments via different channels.

As I continue my journey of life, I keep reminding myself that: "Each adversity, every failure, every heartache carries with it the seed of an equal or greater benefit..." Napoleon Hill. Look for the silver lining as it lies somewhere.

—•••—

REACHING OUT AND LIFTING OTHERS

"I shall pass through this world but once. Any good that I can do, or any kindness that I can show to any human being, let me do it now and not defer it. For I shall not pass this way again"

— Stephen Greeley, French born Quaker

Sometimes we get consumed in our daily routines and we forget what really matters in life. We spend all our time looking for elusive fame, more money, power, higher positions, more influence and material wealth. The list is endless. Before we know it, here comes "time out" and our life here on earth ends.

This is best captured in Luke 12:19-20: "And I will say to my soul: soul you have many goods, stored up for many years, relax, eat, drink and be cheerful." But God said to him: " Foolish one, this very night they require your soul of you. To whom, then will those things belong, which you have prepared?"

And in 1 Corinthians 10:24, St Paul says: "No one should seek their own good but the good of others..."

As such, we should always be guided by the fact that while we have the right to do as we please, we must ask ourselves if everything we engage in is beneficial.

The song "Echo" by Blanca captures the essence of being like Jesus in our interactions with others:

One Thousand four hundred and forty minutes,
Every day I gotta decide
How am gonna live it
I'm gonna take a chance to be the difference
Every day I want to find I'm alive for something....
I made a choice to leave a mark
Carry fire in my heart
No matter where I go...

We should steer away from doing anything that pursues our interests and focus more on acts that build and benefit others. Once we get to that level, we will enjoy true freedom and liberty to do what we should do for others.

Oprah Winfrey once said: "*You cannot continue to succeed in the world and have a fulfilling life unless you choose to use your life in the service of others and give back what you have been given. That's how you keep it. That's how you get it. That's how you grow it!*"

And the late Nobel Laureate, Professor Wangari Maathai, also pointed out that it should not be about what others are doing about a certain situation. It should be about what I can do.

"*Give everything you've got... our small wings are not too small to make a difference. However insignificant in the larger scheme of things, let's do it instead of standing by, watching and complaining and waiting for others to do it. Say instead: 'I will be a hummingbird. I will do the best I can!'*"

In his book "How to Impact and Influence others" James Merritt says " *I can't do anything about your heritage, and neither can you. But you can do something about your legacy*" Sometimes we mistakenly think that we have blown it and that our influence factor and impact ledger are in the negative because of circumstances and events that happened to us. Things like divorce, alcoholism and other addictions, dysfunctional families, public scandals, and even scandalous behaviours in the family that leave scars in our lives might leave us feeling helpless, and think that we have no power to change anything. We cannot change our past, but we can choose to become a power of one person and have a massive impact.

For me, the big question is how will I create and leave a lasting legacy of greatness after I am gone and how to get the best version of myself that makes others happy and grateful for my contributions to their lives and the world at large. The big question, then, is when I die what will my epitaph say?

Steve Jobs reminded us *"If you live each day as if it was the last, someday you'll most certainly be right…"*

This begs the question: How do I find meaning in life? How do I influence the lives of others for the better and reconnect with my purpose?

On July 13, 2022, the Microsoft founder Bill Gates announced that he was on a mission to give out $113 billion to his foundation and eventually drop off the list of the world's richest people altogether.

"I have an obligation to return my resources to society in ways that have the greatest impact on reducing suffering and improving lives. And I hope others in positions of great wealth and privilege will step up at this moment too," he tweeted.

The Bill & Melinda Gates Foundation is already one of the world's largest charitable organisations with a particular focus on finding solutions to global issues like disease, poverty, and climate change, and especially improving access to healthcare and education. He wants his donations to fund research and development on preventing future pandemics, mitigation of climate change and reducing infant mortality from preventable diseases in the near future.

We all need to take responsibility to support disadvantaged members of our society in their quest to lift themselves out of abject poverty.

For me to be able to go through school, I was supported by many people. Part of my school fees was paid through bursaries and generous donations from friends and relatives since my Mum's meagre income as a peasant farmer was hardly enough to educate my five siblings and I.

I, therefore, count it my responsibility to empower others by giving them the fishing rod to become self-reliant. I do not believe in giving people fish since tomorrow they will come for more. Many times, I have turned down requests for short-term assistance since I do not believe in creating a culture of dependency that does not contribute positively to either the giver or the recipient.

It is important to remember that the impact one has on others is largely dependent on one's character. We make a lasting impression on the lives of others by ensuring somebody else sees, hears, or feels real love from us every day either by showing or telling them, and becoming people marked by patience and self-control. In addition, learning the art of being faithful and loyal and dependable to the core is a significant contributing factor to building our own circle of influence and impact.

Let us remember we cannot do kindness too soon as we never know how soon it will be too late. Let us take every opportunity to be kind. My biggest role model for kindness is Jesus Christ as well captured in the Bible in Ephesians 2:6-7: "God raised us up with Christ and seated us with Him in the heavenly realms in Christ Jesus, in order that in the coming ages he might show the incomparable riches of His grace, expressed in kindness to us in Christ Jesus" This means that kindness and eternity are inseparably linked.

━◆••◆━

When I met Yvonne Miteka, I was immediately drawn to her by her radiant smile and zeal to succeed. After finishing her secondary school education, in 2015, she immediately started looking for a job. But armed only with a high school certificate, finding a job is a tall order as she would find out later.

Her parents could not afford to take her to college, weighed down by the burden of paying school fees for her younger siblings with meagre earnings. So, when she reached out to me seeking assistance to further her education, I did not hesitate to step in.

I arranged for her enrolment at Outspan Medical College in Nyeri for a Diploma in Health Records and Information Technology. Over the next one and half years, she would commute to college from my home in Nyeri town. And she did not disappoint! Today, Yvonne is in charge of record keeping at a Hospital in the Nasra area of the sprawling Umoja estate in Nairobi.

She is just one of the many youths I have taken under my initiative of helping young people to become self-reliant by helping them acquire enabling skills in their areas of interest to find employment and earn an income of their own. Because of the great number of those who need help, providing the needed support isn't something I would be able to achieve by myself. I have therefore chosen to seek partners among my contacts within the region and elsewhere to raise funds for such initiatives. Beneficiaries like Yvonne can now help out her parents in paying school fees for her younger siblings.

I am of the view that while money is important, sometimes it takes holding someone's hand and pointing them to the golden door for them to unlock their own potential. There is always a golden door in life, but the problem is that it is sometimes covered in so much soot and darkness that it takes someone getting some vantage point to see it. And for others, it sometimes takes just a word of encouragement to turn their life around.

This is exactly what Hannah Wanjiru Njoroge needed. I learnt of her plight via Facebook. Hannah was dealing with the trauma of an abusive relationship. She had a passion for singing but did not have money for recording some of the songs she had done and posted on Facebook.

When I came across some of her work, I was blown away by her talent and decided to reach out to her. I was convinced that all she needed was the proverbial helping hand. I encouraged her to take guitar and piano lessons at the Conservatoire of Music and also arranged for a vocal trainer to hone her skills alongside four other aspiring musicians at Kamulu on the outskirts of Nairobi.

They all got lessons in music as a business opportunity and were introduced by experienced players in the sector to the intricate details of the industry among other areas. They successfully recorded their first audios in December 2021 and videos shortly thereafter.

Some of my friends and relatives thought I had lost it and went crazy when I told them about the project. "What does this have to do with your career in banking?" they wondered.

Today, Hannah and her colleagues are on the path to becoming the next big thing in the music industry. I can only watch with pride as they deliver their performances. My role is to keep nudging them forward and being their best cheerleader. Watch this space!

➤ •••• ◄

Emotion can inspire and paralyse at the same time.

On February 27, 2021, we set out from Acacia Hotel in Kisumu for Karungu on the southernmost part of Lake Victoria. It was a hot, bright day. As our vehicle tore through the winding roads, we took in the sights, passing through Ahero, Nyakach, Ndhiwa, Homa Bay, Kendu Bay and Rodi Kopany before docking on the shores of Karungu. I was accompanied by a group of some of my friends, including Jemimah Kiarie, George Marenya, my brother Edwin Kibaara and Martin Njuguna, on a visit to Karungu-BL Tezza Special School for the Deaf, which I have been supporting for many years.

I first learnt of the school through Father John Mwai Theuri of the Archdiocese of Nyeri and a lecturer at the Catholic University of Eastern Africa. At the end of 2019, I paid a visit there and got a first-hand account of the story behind the school.

The school for the hearing-impaired was started in 2015 with an initial enrolment of 23 students with the sole mission of providing access to basic education to the beneficiaries. Prior to 2015, the entire Migori and Homa Bay counties and surrounding areas had no special school to cater for learners with hearing difficulties.

Being a boarding school, the new institution also addressed the logistics of such learners having to commute from their homes to the school daily.

As the only school of its kind within an expansive area, it created an upsurge in demand for admissions, thereby putting enormous pressure on the existing infrastructure such as classrooms, dormitories, dining areas and washrooms. The influx of new students meant that some of them had to be accommodated in a neighbouring school.

One of the issues the school administration led by the Chairman Fr Reuben Njagi and the Principal, Madam Millicent Casaines, had to deal with the cultural myths regarding children with hearing impairment, which resulted in stigmatisation and even banishment from the community. It is against this backdrop that I committed to funding the construction of two classrooms. After I made this commitment on the way back home, feelings of doubt engulfed me and I asked myself why I had felt compelled to make such a serious commitment that requires a large amount of cash investment to those children whom I didn't even know. Was this commitment beyond my reach? Had I overstretched myself this time? Was I perhaps biting more than I could chew? I remembered the story of Abraham going to make a sacrifice to the Lord and his son Isaac asked him where the sacrificial lamb was. He simply answered, "The Lord will provide." This is all I needed to clear my feelings of doubt and guilt and after that, it was all systems go.

I contacted some of my friends, raised funds and together we donated books and other items to the school. On this day, we were here to officially hand over the new block of classes that had just been completed and also donate some books. The welcome from the students warmed our hearts as they danced to the beats despite not being able to speak normally or hear.

The boarding school survives on the goodwill of donors. Other well-wishers have come in to support and have donated a dormitory, solar heating and lighting, a water pump and pipes to deliver water from the lake, about 800 metres away. The school too has received support to establish greenhouses to ensure that they grow sufficient food for their consumption instead of being dependent on handouts for food.

After a long but joyous day, at the school, I felt fulfilled and satisfied that I had made a difference! Nothing could ever replace the feeling of happiness and contentment that I felt as I flew back to Nairobi after this event. The beaming faces of the children of Karungu as my friend Jemimah and I sat on the desks in the newly opened classroom is still a memory I cherish to date.

—●●●—

Flame Mentors Group was formed in 2008 by the beneficiaries of the Equity Leaders Programme (ELP), an initiative by Equity Bank to give university scholarships to academically gifted students who topped in their respective districts in the Kenya Certificate of Secondary Education (KCSE). In their own words, they felt obliged to give back to society after Equity Bank took them under its wings for their high school education.

Most of them came from humble backgrounds. After brainstorming on how they could sustainably give back, they settled on a high school mentorship programme aimed at guiding students on academic excellence, career path and character development.

The group's mission resonated with most high school students who had similar experiences. I learnt about the group when I was looking for mentors to accompany me for a motivational talk at my alma mater in 2012. This was so impactful as the school noted a marked improvement in performance and discipline.

I asked the Programme's Chairman, Mr Edwin Mwangi, who is also a tech entrepreneur, how he was able to balance his busy schedule with the demands of mentoring the youth.

This is what he had to say:

"In my over 15 years of mentoring high school students, I have found that mentorship can be motivational or inspirational. Motivation is short-lived but inspiration spurs long-term changes in the character of the student, which leads to success in academic goals and other life goals. I have also found out that as a mentor, sharing real-life stories is more impactful as the students are able to connect and identify with what they are going through and believe that if the mentor overcame his challenges, they too can overcome their own and prosper."

I was sold on the idea, and since then, Flame Mentors have been part of my talking engagements. Some of the mentees who have benefited from the program include Naomi Geita, Edwin Mwangi, Mary Catherine Wanjiku, Wambui Maina, Denis Nyawira, Watson Muturi, Patrick Munuhe and Nelson Mwai.

I have equally benefited from my interactions with them, having stood by me when I lost my Mum in 2017 and following the breakup of my marriage and separation from my ex-husband.

On my 49th birthday, they gave me as a gift *"Option B"*, a book by Sheryl Sandberg, which I read on a flight to Kinshasa for board meetings. It was therapeutic. One of the lessons that I picked from the book is captured in one of the chapters:

"We want others to be happy. Allowing ourselves to be happy- accepting that it is okay to push through the guilt and seek joy- is a triumph over permanence. Having fun is a form of self-compassion; just as we need to be kind to ourselves when we make mistakes, we also need to be kind to ourselves by enjoying life when we can... tragedy breaks down your door and takes you prisoner. To escape takes effort and energy. Seeking joy after adversity is taking back what was stolen from you. Joy is the ultimate act of defiance..."

The team also gifted me other life-changing books like *Lean In* by Sheryl Sandberg, *5 Am Club* by Robin Sharma, *The Hard Thing about Hard Things* by Ben Horowitz, among others.

To propagate various principles of discipline, hard work and integrity and promote a reading culture, I have made it part of my routine to gift books to my mentees depending on their stage in life. I usually require them to share the lessons learnt after reading the books. One such book is *Vitamins of Success* by Mbugua Mumbi.

Others are *Be Inspired Before You Expire* by Pepe Minambo, *Eat That Frog* by Brian Tracy, *The Seven Habits of Highly Successful People* by Steve Covey, *The 8th Habit* by Steve Covey, *Make Your Bed* by Admiral William H McRaven and *Secrets Series* by Rhonda Byrne and several others.

But why spend time and resources on people, some of whom I have never even met?

The simple answer is that I want to become the champion of destiny for as many people as I can, challenging them to be the best they can be and fulfilling their dreams. I have found this very rewarding too.

My Mum's life revolved around prayer, and upholding her strong convictions about the Catholic faith. Cornelia, as she was fondly referred to, believed in the power of prayer in overcoming life's challenges, giving gratitude and drawing one closer to God.

When the missionaries first came to Nyeri in the early 1900s, their first stop was Mununga-ini Catholic Parish. My grandfather Matteo Ng'enda and several others of my ancestors were among the initial converts to Christianity, particularly the Catholic faith in the area.

It followed, therefore, that my Mum embraced the faith from an early age, getting baptised a day after her birth. She was also introduced to a life of prayer at an early age, which became part and parcel of her entire life and which she instilled in us when she became a mother. We had to say prayers, including the rosary, daily before dinner, come rain or shine. Even when my Mum started ailing and came to live with me in Nairobi, she dedicated most of her time to prayer, fasting and meditation.

Mum took every opportunity to remind us of the need to prioritise prayer and seek God at all times. She especially emphasized the role of the Virgin Mary as our intercessor to Jesus and His Father God Almighty in keeping with the teaching and practice of the Roman Catholic Church. To her, praying the holy rosary was a daily requirement irrespective of our circumstances.

So, when she passed on in 2017, my siblings and I decided to build a grotto at the Tetu Catholic Parish, Catholic Archdiocese of Nyeri in her honour, where family members and visitors could offer intercessions through Mother Mary. We felt that the facility would be a befitting gift to the community and in memory of the many church projects she supported. It is a place of pilgrimage, prayer and devotion and one that cements our family's association with the foundation of the church.

Since Maria Consolata was her patron saint and that of the Catholic Women Association, to which she was a faithful member to the end, we named the grotto after the patron saint. Every gift that Mum gave us to mark key occasions in our lives was in one way or another associated with the Maria Consolata patron saint, which made it even more befitting to honour her memory through this gesture.

On the first anniversary of her death in 2018, we were delighted to have the Bishop of the Catholic Diocese of Murang'a, Rt. Rev James Maria Wainaina, supported by the Parish priest, Fr Herman Kiboi, officially dedicate the grotto as a house of prayer to the glory of God.

"The days come and go like muffled and veiled figures sent from a distant friendly party but they say nothing. And if we do not use the gifts they bring, they carry them silently away."

Ralph Waldo Emerson.

DREAM, LIVE AND LEAVE LEGACY

"Do not pray for easy lives, pray to be stronger men"

— John F. Kennedy

On 10th March 2023, I was invited to give the keynote address to young women who had broken barriers in various industries and professions under the *Top40Under40* initiative by the *Nation Media Group*.

I wondered what I would say to these women, who were already successful in their own right. After much thought, I decided to centre my address along three broad themes which are a prerequisite for one to have a full and fulfilling life irrespective of the years lived in this mortal body: living, dreaming and creating a legacy.

⬤ ⦿⦿ ⬤

Building Resilience

I was born in a small village in Nyeri County and my mother was a peasant farmer without much money, and no connections or networks.

Despite my disadvantaged background, I decided that the future would not be a continuation of the past. And therefore, in that regard, there are some choices people like me had to make in life to make the future better. With resilience, resolve and focus, it happened to me. Every human being needs to make a decision to start living.

I decided not to always complain about what I did not have and instead apply the God-given gifts to create a better future for myself and my family. I decided to work toward the life I really wanted. Even back in primary school, I would use every spare minute to study. It did not matter that the only lighting available then was a small smoky paraffin lamp that emitted strong fumes that made my eyes red, watery and painful. It also did not matter that I had no study room or table to make me comfortable while I studied or that the first time I wore shoes was when I joined secondary school. Walking barefoot to school did not deter me from pursuing excellence.

Sometimes we get so engrossed in thinking about our past, complaining about how hard things are and using that as an excuse for our inaction. One mantra that has helped me navigate through life is that my future does not have to be a continuation of the past. I had no control over where I was born or the family I was born into, but by my actions, I could craft a new future for myself and shape my own destiny.

With the support of my mother, who was my greatest cheerleader, I worked hard to get out of the village and thrive by myself.

We do not have to watch our troubles pile up without action. The following story borrowed from *"Dare to Do Motivation"* aptly describes this point.

> *In ancient times, the king had his men place a huge rock on the pathway. He then hid in the bushes and watched to see if anyone would move the rock out of the way. Some of the king's wealthiest merchants and courtiers passed by and simply walked around it. Many people blamed the king for not keeping the road clear. But none of them did anything about getting the stone removed. And so it happened that one day a peasant came along carrying vegetables. Upon approaching the rock, the peasant laid down his burden and tried to push the rock out of the way. After much pushing and straining, he finally managed to remove the rock. After the peasant went back to pick up his vegetables, he noticed a purse lying on the road where the rock had been. The purse contained many gold coins and a note from the king explaining that the gold was for the person who would remove the rock from the road.*

I decided that every obstacle in life would present an opportunity to improve myself and become better every day instead of just sitting idly complaining.

When life pulls us back, it may be preparing to launch us into something great. All we need is to stay focused.

I found favour with many people who supported me in various ways to actualise my dreams. My initial motivation was to move out of the village, but I ended up achieving success and impacting others beyond my wildest imagination.

The renowned retired basketballer, Michael Jordan, once said:

> *"If you are trying to achieve, there will be roadblocks. I've had them. But obstacles don't have to stop you. If you run into a wall, don't turn around and give up. Figure out how to climb it, go through it or work around it."*

I have learnt that sometimes the greatest opportunities are disguised as obstacles, and if we are not careful, we can miss them. I chose to recognise what my talents were and maximised them. I also learnt that I needed to be adaptable. I have seen many people give up on life due to a change in fortunes because of a job loss, the collapse of a business, losing their life savings or any other regrettable life events that happen to us from time to time.

I had to often remind myself that there is no luck without action. In life, lucky breaks are nothing more than the unexpected rewards for the intelligent and deliberate choices you make.

Further, I realised that success does not just happen because one's stars are aligned. I had to work overtime many times to get to where I am today. Rising to the level of Group Executive Director in the largest financial services group in the region was no mean feat for a poor village girl. It called for sacrifice, hard work and focus through and through.

When Mary, Mother of Jesus, told Him that they had run out of wine in the story of the wedding in Cana in the Bible (John 2:1-12). In response, He instructed the hosts to fill up the wine jars with water. Only then did the water turn into wine. For a miracle to happen, therefore, we must first take action.

—•••—

Power of purpose

When I joined Equity Building Society, it could not join the Clearing House and could not do settlements with other banks. It needed to use another Bank to be its Banker. At that time, it was ranked last in size and performance in the industry. My first task was the conversion of the Building Society to a Commercial Bank.

Our team leader, Dr James Mwangi addressed us one day when we were preparing for the cutover date. "In the next five years, Equity will be bigger than all the banks in this country [Kenya]," said Dr Mwangi. Compared to other players in the market at the time, it looked like a pipe dream, but this inspired me to change the status quo.

I worked hard to deliver on all my assignments. Speedy and seamless execution became a habit in Equity for all team members.

There were many naysayers in the marketplace, those who expected the business model adopted by Equity Bank to fail. Some said you cannot possibly give loans to low-income earners and stay sustainably profitable. The Equity Business model was a first; hence, many people did not quite understand how it worked or how the commercial engine worked. The model is a low-margin, high volume where the unit cost of operation is distributed among several consumers, making the bank affordable. Because of its uniqueness, many people initially expected it to fail.

It reminded me of a quote by Friedrich Nietzsche: *"And those who were seen dancing were thought to be insane by those who could not hear the music."*

In life and at work, we should not be deterred and derailed by busybodies, who have no clue why we do what we do the way we do it. I completely blocked out their negative energy.

I learnt that to achieve my dreams, I had to internalise them, and put all the requisite efforts in their fulfilment. Instead of saying "I can't do it," I ask myself; "How can I do this?" and this mindset has made all the difference in my life.

I have also learnt that one should not be afraid of failing or walking the road less travelled.

Equity was declared technically insolvent within the first 10 years of its formation in 1984 because of adopting a similar business model to its rivals. It took the bold step of overhauling its business model to break even. We had to sail out of the red ocean and swim into the blue ocean. By 2010, Equity became the largest bank by customer base, shareholders return and second in asset size and profitability.

The entire process taught me to be passionate about what I do while being cautiously optimistic about the likely outcome.

━ ••• ━

Opening the golden door

> " *Let your soul expand, let your heart reach out to others in loving and generous warmth, and great and lasting will be your joy, and all prosperity will come to you....*"

James Allen

A story is told about how Mahatma Gandhi once boarded a train and one shoe slipped and fell on the track. Since the train was in motion, he could not retrieve it. To the consternation of his fellow passengers, he took the remaining shoe and threw it back to land close to the first. When asked why he did so he said: "*The poor man who finds the shoes lying on the track will now have a pair he can use.*"

The more I speak with the young people that I sponsor through college or university, the more I realise the importance of the role of mentorship in nurturing their dreams. I insist on seeing their end-of-term results or transcripts to see how they are faring in their studies.

When following up with these students on their performance in school, I realised that one of the girls had fallen into bad company and was convinced that the school she was in was the problem.

I had a candid conversation with her, drawing from my life story about how I ended up at Tetu Boys' Primary School, taking cold showers every morning in high school and surviving on a diet that even prisoners today would frown upon. After this conversation, her perspective on life changed, and there was a marked improvement in her grades.

Acts of kindness should not be done for recognition and publicity. Giving unconditionally to people who can never pay us back leads to a more fulfilling life. After all, as the legendary former American President Abraham Lincoln put it, "*In the end, it's not the years in your life that count: it's the life in your years*".

One major life lesson I have come to appreciate is that winning is not everything. Sometimes how you run the race is more important. There is no value in greatness if you cannot lift others up.

I have chosen not to be like a tall tree that cannot give shade to anyone and its fruits are out of reach, but to share the joy of my success with others. I believe that I would not be where I am today if others had not lent me a hand. As I pursue my goals as a leader, I always want to understand how I can use my competencies to uplift others and make a difference in the broader society.

Love, care, and compassion are the essence of our being, and I aspire to make this a daily habit by being kind to others.

The question I always ask myself at the end of the day is whether I am impacting others positively through my actions or not.

"At the end of the day, it's not about what you have or even what you've accomplished... It's about who you've lifted, who you've made better. It's about what you have given back."

- Denzel Washington

But make no mistake, giving is not just about a big cheque or cash donation. It is sometimes about a word of encouragement or a simple act of kindness to someone going through a rough time or being there for a friend who lost someone special.

➤ ••• ◀

Never Ever Give Up on Your Dreams

In 2008 after a capital injection by Helios Investors of about $185 million, Equity embarked on regional expansion to the rest of the East African region as part of the vision of empowering the continent. As the Director of Strategy, I oversaw the successful acquisition of Uganda Microfinance Limited.

But within two years of commencing operations, it was clear that something was amiss. The unit's non-performing loan portfolio was incredibly high, deposits had stagnated, and incidents of fraud reported undermined the brand image and overall performance. We could not attract the right people to the bank due to bad publicity and poor financial performance.

I was at a loss about what had gone wrong. Pressure started mounting from the board to make it work or exit the market. I carried the heavy burden of the nagging thought of ever again facing our investors to seek approval to implement any other investment in the region.

Rather than give up, I decided to stick to my honour and tried to understand what had gone wrong and determine a fitting corrective action to achieve success. I had to remind myself that failure is part of success. After overhauling the governance structures, re-engineering business processes and changing the management, the Ugandan business became one of the best-performing subsidiaries of the Group!

The words of Admiral William McLaren in *Make Your Bed* still ring true:

> "*In SEAL training (in the navy) there is a bell that hangs in the centre of the compound for all to see. All you have to do to quit is ring the bell. Ring the bell and you no longer have to wake up at 5 o'clock. Ring the bell and you no longer have to do the freezing cold swims. Ring the bell and you no longer have to do the runs, the obstacle course or endure the hardships of training. Just ring the bell,*" he writes.

We decided not to ring the bell but to hold on and do what needed to be done to turn around the business. If we had given up, we would have missed the opportunities that came with regional expansion.

Sometimes in our jobs, business undertakings and other endeavours, we are tested to the limit. It is even worse when our teachers, friends, family, colleagues or even strangers keep on telling us that we were not cut out for success.

We may have at one time in our lives been told we shall not amount to anything, among other words of discouragement. Some individuals do everything in their power to embarrass and taunt us, giving us enough reason to throw in the towel.

But we must never forget that life is full of difficulties and disappointments. We must remember that there is always someone out there having it worse. Do not allow yourself to wallow in self-pity, sorrow, anger or regret. Do not get into a blame game.

My job at Equity Bank is not easy. I have to wake up early at 4.45 am daily to get to the office by 6.45 am. Other times, I have to stay up all night to beat deadlines, while Board meetings sometimes go up to 8 pm.

Every quarter, I have to travel to five countries in the region for board meetings, which is quite taxing. But looking at where we have come from - a technically insolvent Building Society with 27 employees and negative shareholders' funds to the largest financial institution serving over 18 million customers spread over six regional countries and a balance sheet of over $13 billion - gives me the strength and the drive to soldier on.

Come to think of it, if the founders of Equity Bank gave up when it was declared insolvent and condemned for closure by the Central Bank of Kenya in the early 90s, I would not be in Equity today. Instead of throwing in the towel, they chose to plead their case to the regulator and were reluctantly given another chance. Dr James Mwangi chose to give up a sterling career as a financial controller in another financial institution to take up the turnaround challenge in a company whose future was anything, but rosy. The rest, as they say, is history.

Do not quit!

→ ••• ←

Be authentic

One thing I vowed to myself when I started my career was to be true to myself, standing for the truth even when it is unpopular to do so. This is the essence of being authentic. Authenticity comes at a cost because sometimes we are judged by others as being stupid, difficult or even harsh.

Refusing to "play ball" may mean losing out on certain "deals." However, in the long run, it earns you respect and trust and allows you to be fully in control of your life. This kind of approach has earned me a reputation within the bank for being a no-nonsense leader.

But with time, it has silenced the murmurs of disapproval that existed when I first joined the bank for saying no to some requests, insisting on the right documentation. My colleagues have grown to trust me, realising it is sometimes for their protection and also for the good of our common stakeholders.

→ ••• ←

Be a person of integrity

I deliberately avoid any relationship that might run counter to my principles of integrity. I have resisted the temptation to enter into "arrangements" with customers or suppliers to the bank. This helps a lot, especially when I need to make decisions since I do not feel pressured to act in a certain way.

Sometime back when I was the Company Secretary, a certain service provider sued the Bank for alleged breach of contract. He then sent a close friend of mine to talk to me with a view to reaching a settlement. I had earlier read the file and concluded that it was a case that the bank needed to defend to the end.

Sending my friend was meant to compromise my position, which I resisted. I sent my friend back to tell him to speak to our lawyers, after which they would advise the Bank on the way forward. He was not amused. He wrote a letter to the Group Managing Director, complaining about how unreasonable I was. In the letter, he said he had never met "a Company Secretary as stupid as that one of your bank."

When I explained to my senior what had transpired, he encouraged me to remain firm on my decision.

The reality is that sometimes our colleagues, family, friends and society may castigate and mock us and even judge us harshly for doing the right thing. We, therefore, must have a very strong resolve to remain steadfast and true to our ethical campus. We have to walk the straight and narrow path and even withstand some amount of ridicule to achieve excellence!

Encounters such as the one I went through might trigger feelings of inadequacy in our capabilities. I must admit I suffer from imposter syndrome once in a while. However, I try to conquer it by first understanding how and why these feelings come about. I have to keep reminding myself that I have earned my place at the table, it didn't come on a silver platter!

I always celebrate every milestone in my journey, which helps me to internalise the fact that I deserve to be where I am. I also avoid downplaying my success without necessarily being arrogant about it, and where I fall short, I use that as an opportunity to learn and grow instead of beating myself too hard.

Loss, grief and failure are part of success

In 2016, I struggled with my conscience before ending my 25-year marriage, navigating through a breakup and eventually in divorce. Seeds of doubt and loss of willpower engulfed me. For the life of me, I could not understand how I completed so many mega transactions for the bank, yet failed in one of the most important areas of my personal life.

I was on the verge of an emotional and physical breakdown. I sought answers in books, documentaries, the Bible and The Canon Law (a Code for Roman Catholics). Uncertainty about the future kept pulling me back until I came across this famous quote from the Inspirational Quotes Journal that strengthened me:

> *"When people make you feel unwanted… don't leave to make them feel sad or guilty, they won't. Leave them because you no longer have a reason to stay. Sometimes you have to be strong for yourself. What is meant to be will end up good and what is not- won't. Love is worth fighting for, but sometimes you can't be the only one fighting. At times, people need to fight for you. If they don't, you just have to move on and realise what you gave them was more than they were willing to give you."*

I realised that I needed to handle difficult moments in a way that eventually would lead me to appreciate the big picture. I had to seek professional help to deal with the negative emotions that I was going through at the time. It took me a while to accept that I needed help and sought the support of a psycho-social therapist, who told me the truth and not what I wanted to hear.

Eventually, I got to a point where I could celebrate and live my life to the fullest. I overcame the anger, bitterness and sadness that had paralysed me and sprang into action to put our life back on track.

➤•••◆

Be Effective, not busy!

Time isn't the main thing. It's the only thing - Miles Davis

I wake up at 4.45 am daily. I exercise or meditate before getting ready to leave the house by 6.15 am. I get to the office at 6.45 am, which gives me time to work quietly before people start streaming into my office and start demanding my time. I believe in the adage… *"early to bed, early to rise, makes someone healthy and wealthy and wise."*

Time is the most valuable free resource that we have in life. If we lose time, we can never replace it like we do other material possessions. I strive to account for every minute of my life by prioritising the most important tasks. I execute the most unpleasant tasks first while still fresh and energetic.

Procrastination is a thief of time and stops us from achieving our objectives. I do everything with a sense of urgency. Of course, the danger with this kind of approach is that one runs the risk of making the wrong decisions. But over time, I have learnt that it is better to make the wrong decision than no decision at all. That way, you know what works and what does not work. My Group Managing Director, Dr Mwangi, constantly reminds us that not deciding on any issue is a decision in itself.

People I have worked closely with tell me I walk very fast. It is true since once I decide I need to be in a certain place, why waste time dragging my feet to get there?

I try not to clutter my life with tasks that can be delegated to others. I live my life as if every day were the last day of my life.

I set my goals with clarity and then have a plan of action. Every year, for as long as I can remember, I have a personal development or investment project that I must accomplish. In December, I review the progress. The goals vary from small ones like finishing a book to big ones like buying a new car, building a car shade for my parking, building a house or investing in shares.

Back in 1995, I agonised over leaving employment and starting my own legal practice. Though I struggled initially, I later felt that it was the right decision to plunge into the unknown. I was still young then and had a whole future ahead of me to correct any mistakes that I made.

Action without planning is a sure recipe for failure. Similarly, planning without action will not achieve any results.

—●••●—

Love yourself

"We are incapable of loving another unless we love ourselves, just as we are incapable of teaching our children self-discipline unless we, ourselves, are self-disciplined. It is actually impossible to forsake our own spiritual development in favour of someone else's. We cannot forsake self-discipline and at the same time be disciplined in our care for another. We cannot be a source of strength unless we nurture our own strength. I believe that not only do self-love and love of others go hand in hand but that ultimately, they are indistinguishable." Scott Peck, *The Road Less Travelled*

Taking time to recharge while doing something I love brings some rhythmic pattern to my life. I love taking a leisurely walk, getting on the exercise bike, and listening to music (especially from the 70s and 80s).

In life, everything that happens has a purpose, however unpleasant. I can only give what I have. If I am exhausted, I will have nothing to give to others. If I am stressed, I will give back stress. If I am happy, I will spread happiness to all I interact with. I make a conscious effort to keep a positive attitude. I strive to improve every aspect of my being - mind, body and spirit.

I have learnt to always be grateful to God and others for the seemingly small pleasures of life. For instance, I am grateful to Emma Wasilwa, who manages my diary and helps me organise board meetings for our regional subsidiaries. And what would I do without Juliet Nekesa, who keeps my house in order and prepares a hot cup of tea for me after a hard day's work, ensures there is milk in the fridge and the children have eaten even when I am away. There is also Gilbert Opwaka, who keeps the garden impeccably neat and Elizabeth Aluoch, who has taken care of my hair for more than a decade, not forgetting Jackie Mugo, my spa therapist, who calls me if I miss my monthly appointments.

"It's a funny thing about life, once you begin to take note of the things you are grateful for, you begin to lose sight of the things that you lack."

— Germany Kent

Anchor your life on the love of God and others

As far as I can remember, my Mum never missed mass even once. She would make us recite daily prayers and the Holy Rosary before dinner.

She also instilled the discipline of prayer and thanksgiving. I donate to church projects just like she used to do because I am a firm believer in the biblical teaching that "it is more blessed to give than to receive."

Love is a crucial element in the search for personal and professional success. The greatest teacher of love was Jesus himself. When tested by a scholar of the law about what was the greatest commandment, He did not hesitate to lay down the rule: "Love the Lord your God with all your heart, and with all your soul and with all your mind," closely followed by: "Love your neighbour as yourself." (Matthew 22:35-40)

Love sets off a divine chain reaction and kindles the fire of compassion, which leads to service. This, in turn, creates hope that results in faith, which is a true reflection of the glory and power of God.

Love should go hand in hand with the fear of the Lord, which is the beginning of wisdom. It is more about respect and reverence for God than actual fear in its modern definition. The fear of God is knowing God. Therein lies true wisdom. The book of Proverbs also teaches that we must submit to God's will. By doing so, we acquire wisdom.

With this in mind, I have recently re-dedicated myself to live the fruit of the Holy Spirit. That is love, joy, peace, patience, kindness, goodness, faithfulness, gentleness and self-control so as to find favour with God and fellow humans.

Finally, I embrace these three simple rules of life:

1. If you don't go after what you want in life, you will never get it.

2. If you don't ask, the answer will always be NO.

3. If you don't step forward, you're always in the same spot.

IN THEIR WORDS

*"Develop an attitude of gratitude and give thanks
for everything that happens to you, knowing that
every step forward is a step toward achieving
something bigger and better than your current
situation."*

— Brian Tracy

Mathew Ng'enda, Mary's elder brother, loves a good laugh. The second-born among the six siblings has an infectious laugh and a likeable demeanour.

Mary had spoken glowingly of him, and when it was his turn to talk about his little sister, it was obvious to see how strong their bond is.

With six years between them, Mathew was way ahead of Mary in school, but he always looked out for his little sister, whom he fondly refers to as Wangari. Mary describes him as a father figure and mentor to his younger siblings, filling the void of growing up without a father around.

From accounts of her older siblings, Mathew had a knack for getting into trouble and one time insulted a teacher back in primary school, which earned him the beating of a lifetime from their mother.

Mary's story would not have been complete without the input of the man who witnessed first-hand her rise to the top from their humble beginnings in Tetu.

When Mathew sat down to give his account of being a big brother to Mary, he could not do so without first telling the story of their dear late mother.

From his narration, the influence she had on him and his other siblings is evident, helping them overcome a painful past founded on a bitter family feud that had threatened to ruin generations of the Ng'enda lineage.

Mathew speaks with ease and the confidence of a man who has seen it all, his narration punctuated by funny anecdotes and bouts of laughter.

But when he starts to trace the roots of his family during the Mau Mau uprising against the British colonialists, his solemn voice betrays the pain of many descendants of the freedom fighters who did not benefit from the struggle for independence, with the spoils going to the collaborators.

"Was I affected by the Mau Mau rebellion? Yes, in the sense that where I was born in the upper side of Tetu, most of the families or our parents were in the forest fighting or would take food to the Mau Mau. My mother was part of the team that took food every day to the forest," says Mathew.

"They [the colonialists] decided to put everyone else in concentration camps so that they did not have time to take food to Mau Mau fighters."

The war meant that his mother and many other individuals involved in the struggle either directly or indirectly did not get the opportunity to go to school.

"When most of our parents came back from the forest, they did not have land, and their children did not go to school. So, when the war ended, we became squatters," says Mathew. But on the other end of the spectrum, the collaborators were rewarded with huge tracts of land and good jobs, while their children attended the best schools in the land.

He gives the example of two of his uncles, one of whom became a teacher and the other a manager at Kenya Railways. "They became somebody in society, while the rest had nothing," says Mathew.

He was part of the generation that was born into poverty as seeds of discord took root over land and other resources in Central Kenya, pitting family members against each other. The Ng'enda family was no exception. The bitter feud over ancestral land threatened to tear the family asunder were it not for the wisdom of his mother and Mathew's leadership.

He says trouble for his family began when his mother returned home with six children following the end of her marriage. His uncles did not take it very well and made no effort to hide their hostility towards her and her children as they saw them as a threat in the land inheritance equation.

With the family patriarch Ng'enda Makara, his grandfather after whom he was named, out of the picture, their mother was left at the mercy of her brothers. Back then, it was unheard of for women to inherit land.

"There was conflict throughout. It affected her completely. She never felt a sense of belonging," says Mathew.

Mary found herself in this complex family matrix that from an early age provided an extra motivation to change her lot in life. It is a motivation that Mathew shared in, especially finding a way to deal with the land dispute with his uncles and cousins.

Their mother was alive to her children's disadvantaged position and emphasised the importance of education in helping them change their situation. "My mother used to tell us if you have no education, you have nothing. She would say: 'I have no land to give you, study and buy yours'," recalls Mathew.

And so, when Mary became a lawyer, Mathew says it was a turning point for the family because she could now offer legal advice and the necessary resources to sway things in their favour. He says when Mary graduated from the University of Nairobi, it was one of the happiest days of his mother's life. "It was the one time I saw my mother really happy. She was the picture of contentment".

Mathew says he is not surprised by Mary's rise to the top despite their humble upbringing. From an early age, he says, she set herself apart as an achiever through sheer hard work and dedication to everything she set out to do.

Mathew describes Mary as generous and kind, saying fame and fortune have not changed her. "Despite coming that far, it has not changed her. If you look back, you see God's hand in her life", he says.

Mathew says despite the difference in their age, they have always been close, with the love for their late mother being a uniting factor. While she spent her last years with Mary, he was actively involved in taking care of her, although he lives miles away in Murang'a and would have long conversations about her last wishes whenever he visited.

He recalls how his mother would constantly urge him to take care of his younger sister while emphasising the need for her children to reconcile with the rest of the extended family. "My mother really wanted to reconcile with the rest of the family even in her last days," says Mathew. Mathew with the help of Mary took up their mother's challenge to bring the family together.

Mathew hails Mary's dedication to caring for their mother in her final years, terming her a pillar in the family for her selflessness in helping others.

He says he had been imploring her to write a book about her life story for years and is happy she finally did it, hoping it would inspire others facing similar challenges to the ones she did to realise their dreams.

Mathew credits Mary with how things worked out in resolving the family dispute despite him taking the lead as the firstborn in his family with the guidance of their mother. Her legal advice, he says, was invaluable. By the time their Mum died, the land dispute had been resolved, and in keeping with her final wishes, she was laid to rest in her ancestral land in Tetu.

And with their differences now behind them, the entire extended family consults Mary on legal matters, which she gladly helps with, all thanks to the values their late mother instilled in them.

"She gave us a strong Christian background. Wangari today is the legal adviser in the extended family", says Mathew proudly.

◼•••◼

Mary's other elder cousin, Father John Baptista Gichuhi, a Catholic priest, describes her as open, sincere and always ready to help others.

"She believes we are all born with tremendous natural capacities, and she does not want to lose touch with hers", he says.

Father Gichuhi also attests to Mary's dedication to her work, saying her work ethic is borne out of her love for what she does rather than money. "She does her work out of conviction and not out of convenience", he says.

About her relationship with her late mother, Father Gichuhi describes their relationship as special, saying Mary would go out of her way to make sure she was comfortable. "She really loved her and would do anything for her".

Asked if any of her siblings ever imagined she would become as successful as she is today, Father Gichuhi says he never doubted Mary's ability to succeed in life. He says Mary excelled in her studies from primary to university, which gave her an edge over others. "She is what she is today because of her dedication and commitment", says Father Gichuhi, adding that her resilience has also helped her with challenges that would, otherwise, break many people.

He says success has not changed Mary in any way but has helped her to be more compassionate about the plight of others. "I would say success has made her even more humble and is always ready to help those in need both within the family and society in general", says Father Gichuhi.

Mary rarely misses family gatherings unless she has travelled for work. Father Gichuhi says her concern for others is demonstrated by wanting to know how they are doing and lending a hand where possible.

"We treat Mary with respect not because of her success but because of her love and concern for every member of our family", he says, adding that her down-to-earth demeanour makes her approachable and easy to talk to.

—•••—

When Mary joined Kangubiri Girls', she only had one mission on her mind - to excel in her studies and move onto the next level of her schooling life. She was not what one would call popular, preferring to keep a low profile. But her academic exploits made her known to the rest of the school. According to her long-time friend Sister Rose Catherine Wakibiru, a Catholic nun with Assumption Sisters of Nairobi, Mary hated the limelight, but it always seemed to seek her out.

When Catherine joined Kangubiri Girls', Mary was a class ahead in Form Two despite being two years her junior. "I was a slow learner", explains Sister Catherine. It was the school tradition for the best-performing students to be feted at the end of the term before the entire school. Mary was always top of her class and would be among the students to receive accolades every term. That is how she became popular with the rest of the students.

"Wangari was not noisy like the rest of us. She was known by everyone not because of the noise but for her academic performance", says Sister Catherine.

She recalls how at one time her class teacher, Mr Gikonyo "Sorino", who also doubled up as the music teacher, introduced her as she walked to the front to receive her prize for being the best student that term.

"And here comes Wangari Cornelia, the lawyer", she remembers Mr Gikonyo saying amid applause from the rest of the school. "This girl is going to become a lawyer", he said, not knowing that his prediction about her future career path would come to pass.

When Catherine joined the school, Mary was already the treasurer of the Catholic Action and was the one who welcomed her to the religious organisation that would later nurture her ambitions of becoming a Catholic nun. That is how their friendship began and would last for the rest of their time at Kangubiri and thereafter.

Catherine was amazed by how Mary breezed through her studies without too much effort like the rest of them, alluding to her brilliance from an early age. She recalls how they had to burn the midnight oil studying, dipping their feet in cold water to stay awake. Mary was always a top student and received several accolades for top performance.

Mary's leadership skills and compassion for others started to show at an early age. Catherine remembers how she rallied other girls in her dormitory to come to the aid of one of them when they noticed she did not have shoes and other essentials such as bathing soap and a change of clothes.

"When I was in Form Two, I became a prefect. At some stage, I noticed one of the girls [in my dormitory] did not have shoes. I didn't know how to help her. It's Wangari who advised me to ask the others to contribute items for her. It worked very well. The idea came from her", says Catherine.

Her selflessness was also demonstrated when, during one of the school tours to Nairobi, Mary suggested that instead of buying snacks with the little money they had, they buy some utensils for their families back home.

"I bought a jug, while she bought cups. That particular jug was very prestigious to have in any home at the time", says Catherine. "Such was Mary's character, always thinking of how she could be of help to others".

Catherine also describes Mary as a true friend who did not judge her or others. This came out during a visit to Sr Catherine's home, which was about a two-hour walk from the school.

During public holidays, the girls would be allowed to leave the school in the morning and come back by five o'clock. They would get home and find arrowroots and a hot cup of tea made by Catherine's Mum. "We would make chapatis and sukuma wiki (kales) and enjoy them on the banks of Gura River before hurrying back to school," recalls Catherine.

Catherine also marvels at Mary's unassuming nature, recalling how for almost four years she never disclosed the fact that the priest who conducted mass at the school every Sunday was her cousin Father Mathew Theuri! "I came to learn of it long after I had left Kangubiri. If it were some of us, we would have shouted about it", says Catherine.

When Mary left Kangubiri in 1985, the two friends lost touch for over 10 years. It was by sheer luck that they reconnected through Mary's big brother Mathew Ng'enda. At the time, Catherine had relocated to Murang'a and was staying at a convent near Mathew's home. Mathew's children would pass by the convent after church for snacks offered by the sisters.

One day, they were left behind and their father offered to pick them up later, but they insisted that one of the sisters would bring them home. Catherine offered to drop them off, and after entering the house, she noticed photos of Mary on the walls, including one of her graduation from the University of Nairobi.

She was pleasantly surprised. Mathew could not help noticing the surprise on her face and asked her: "Do you know her?"

"Yes, that was my best friend Wangari back in high school!" she exclaimed.

And so began the journey of reconnecting the two friends. They would link up later in Nairobi, and their friendship flourished more than before, with Catherine finally meeting Mary's Mum, whom she says became a good friend and like a second mother to her.

Over the years, Catherine says she has come to appreciate their friendship more, especially with Mary's change in status. She says fame and money have only changed her for the better as she uses her new-found status to impact others positively.

Catherine witnessed this first-hand sometime in August 2016 when she was about to leave for Jamaica for a three-year church programme. The day before her flight, Mary rang her up. She said she would drop by her house for breakfast the following morning.

After breakfast, she handed her an envelope. "I was sent by Mum and the rest of the family to give you this to buy soda along the way", said Mary. Catherine took the envelope and thanked her before bidding her goodbye. She did not open the envelope until much later when she was about to leave to catch her flight.

She was taken aback by the number of crisp dollar notes stacked up in the envelope. A quick calculation revealed that the money amounted to over Ksh200,000. Still in shock, Catherine called Mary.

"I think you gave me the wrong envelope", she told her, trying to catch her breath.

"What makes you think I gave you the wrong envelope?" posed Mary calmly.

"The money is too much", answered Catherine. "No, it is yours. Mum said we buy you tea and give you pocket money for the years you will be in Jamaica", said Mary.

Catherine was still not convinced. In her admission, she says she expected between Ksh2,000 and Ksh10,000. Mary sought to calm her nerves nonchalantly saying: "It's not a big deal. I was told to bring you the money to buy tea and for your upkeep while in Jamaica".

That act of generosity has stayed with her to this day, although she would experience many others over the years, including Mary's family mobilising funds to buy a bus for her parish when two of their vehicles were stolen.

To sum up her opinion of Mary, Catherine describes her as a "silent influencer" and a kind soul who will go out of her way to help those in need. "She is able to influence people's lives quietly in her own way. She has never changed".

➤●●●➤

Mary's other close friend from high school, Lucy Wangari Irungu, for her part, speaks of the lasting impact their interaction at Ngandu Girls', now Bishop Gatimu Girls', had on her life.

When Mary joined the prestigious school for her A-levels after leaving Kangubiri, Lucy was doing her O-levels. At the time, she recalls, Mary's first cousin, Father J B Gichuhi, was a chaplain at the school and because of her involvement in Catholic Action, she got to know him well.

"I happened to have come from a dysfunctional family, and I used to talk to him about it a lot", says Lucy of how she became close to Mary's cousin.

During one of their many interactions, Father Gichuhi told Mary: "There is a little girl who will be joining the school, I know her. Take care of her". Initially, he did not disclose that she was his cousin and neither did Mary when 'the little girl' reported to the school.

When the new students finally arrived, Lucy sought out Mary and took her under her wing, although A-level students were senior to those in O-level.

"We hit it off like we had known each other forever, but she ended up taking care of me instead", says Lucy of their initial meeting.

She recalls how A-level students were accorded special privileges such as electric kettles to heat their bathing water, iron boxes and special meals, including buttered bread and meat. They also had their own dormitories, library and designated sidewalks to boot!

Despite these privileges and Lucy having been at the school longer, Mary ended up being the one who took Lucy under her wing. "She would bring me some of the buttered bread they used to get and even iron my clothes", says Lucy.

Because Lucy was at the tail end of her O-level studies, their interaction was short-lived, lasting about three terms. But during that time, she says, she noticed Mary's dedication to her studies and Catholic Action (CA). "You would never find her loitering around. She would encourage me to work hard and was very committed to CA", recalls Lucy.

Because of the situation back home, Lucy dreaded school holidays and midterm breaks. Mary suggested she accompany her home instead of being left in school. That is how she got to meet Mary's family, building a lasting bond with them, especially her late mother.

During these visits, she says she noticed how strict Mary's Mum was. With her, there was no partiality, especially when it came to house chores. "It didn't matter if you were a visitor, you had to toe the line. If it was farm work or fetching firewood, everyone had to do their fair share", says Lucy.

She also recalls Mary's Mum's dedication to prayers, with the family praying together after supper every evening.

After high school, they lost contact for a while until they reconnected at university. Their time on campus, says Lucy, was typical of many young women, marked by fun outings and gossip about the opposite sex.

She says Mary is the only friend from high school she has stayed in touch with, speaking to the value both of them place on their friendship.

After campus, they each got engrossed in their respective careers and family life, and it was much later that Lucy would come to know of Mary's high-flying career in the banking sector.

She says one of the most striking aspects of Mary's personality is her ability to keep a low profile despite being a public figure and always having time for those close to her.

She recalls how she helped out with the admission of her son to his preferred school after she had exhausted all avenues she knew of. Her son had been admitted to Othaya Boys' High School, but his mind was set on joining Nyeri High School. After grappling with the issue for a while and with her son on the verge of suffering a major nervous breakdown, Lucy reached out to Mary.

"She gave me an appointment for a particular day, and when I went to see her, she handed me the admission letter to Nyeri High", remembers an emotional Lucy.

"I have no idea where it came from. That is the kind of person Mary is".

She also marvels at Mary's ability to remember people's names even in a large gathering, which she notes is a testimony of her love and genuine concern for others. "You could be in a gathering of 100 people, but she will address everyone by name. I don't know how she does it, but it says a lot about her character", says Lucy.

She also hails her love for mentoring the youth, noting her influence on her son, who was recently admitted to the bar. She remembers one time when he was struggling with one of the units in law school. Mary had a heart-to-heart with him, which helped him refocus his priorities and ended up passing exceptionally well.

Lucy also shares Sister Catherine's view about Mary's unassuming nature, noting how she will hardly use her position to get ahead. "That humility is up there. You wouldn't tell of her position. She does not flaunt it, and not many people know she works at the bank [Equity]", says Lucy.

Her parting shot? "Mary is very realistic about things. She tells it as it is but will give you a chance to argue your case. Her loyalty to friends is through and through".

━●●●●━

For her part, Virginia Wanjiru has known Mary for more than 30 years, first meeting her in their Tetu backyard when she was a child.

She remembers how Mary would come bearing gifts for the neighbourhood children whenever she visited from Nairobi. This earned her the nickname *"cucu wa Nairobi"*(grandmother from Nairobi).

Virginia describes Mary as a generous and kind soul, who is always ready to help others. She took her in after high school in 2005 and lived with her for more than 10 years. "She nurtured me and treated me with kindness without any discrimination", says Virginia of her time living with Mary.

She not only paid for her secondary education but also sponsored her for a Bachelor's degree in commerce at Strathmore University as well as a course in Certified Public Accountant (CPA). Mary later helped Virginia get her first job as an accountant, which set her on the path to financial freedom.

She instilled financial discipline in her, advising her to invest in shares, something Virginia says has paid off big time over the years. "She referred me to Equity's Custody Manager George Mwangi who guided me on how to open a Central Depository and Settlement Corporation (CDSC) account and buy shares.

That is how my investment journey began. The discipline of investing grew, and that is how I made my first three million shillings", says Virginia.

━●●●━

For Catherine Musakali, Mary is the consummate professional. Catherine first met Mary more than 25 years ago at an Institute of Certified Secretaries of Kenya event where she was giving a talk on corporate governance.

She recalls the aplomb with which she delivered her speech and the respect she commanded from her peers. "I was taken in by her knowledge of the subject of corporate governance and collegiality in how she interacted with the rest of the members", says Catherine.

She decided she was worth knowing, and thus began a lifelong friendship and professional relationship that is almost clocking three decades now. "As a company secretary, I needed to know this girl; I needed to do what she was doing", says Catherine of their initial encounter.

She says the most striking thing about Mary from this and subsequent interactions is her professionalism.

Mary, Catherine notes, also has a way of drawing people in with her disarming smile. "Mary has this smile that draws you to her, and you want to discover what is behind this smile", says Catherine. "She is now one of our mentors at the Women on Boards Network that I chair", adds Catherine

Away from her professional life, Catherine says Mary is compassionate about other people's plight and will go out of her way to help those in need, with both of them involved in different causes. "Mary is all about service and giving back. A lot of the work I have done with Mary has been about giving back. Service for humanity is a quality I see in Mary."

→ ••• ←

This aspect of giving is something Catherine Nyambura can attest to.

Nyambura was in Form Three at Gikumbo Secondary School in Mathira Constituency, Nyeri County when she became pregnant with twins in 2010. The untimely pregnancy forced her to drop out of school, dealing a big blow to her academic journey. After delivery, she resigned herself to her fate of becoming a teenage mother.

Because of her family's financial struggles, now worsened by the burden of raising twins, she had no hope of ever going back to school. Nyambura also did not know how to handle the stigma associated with teenage pregnancy if she ever went back to school.

Mary happened to learn of her situation and reached out to her through an acquaintance in her village. "Mary kept on looking for me after hearing of this bright girl who had dropped out of school, and by God's grace located me", says Nyambura.

The logical arrangement would be for her to go to a day school nearby so that she would take care of her babies after school, but Nyambura knew her continued presence at home would only fuel the village gossip mill besides distracting her from her studies.

"I didn't want anything to do with a day school because of what had happened to me", she says.

And so, Mary gave her a choice of choosing where she wanted to go to school. Nyambura opted for Magutu Girls' Secondary School, and Mary paid her fees even though she was yet to meet her in person.

"I met her way later when she came to the school, and we had a brief chat along the corridors. She encouraged me to work hard", says Nyambura.

She says she was struck by her "big heart" and will be eternally grateful for altering the cause of her life by not only encouraging her to go back to school but also for unfailingly paying her school fees. Her parting shot?

"She is a blessing", says Nyambura. "Mary is not interested in being noticed in public, but she remains a force to reckon with and a role model to young women who wish to go far in life".

"She supported me through a nursing course in Kenya Medical Training Centre and am now a qualified nurse. I am able to support my children and extended family"

——•••—

For her part, Wambui Maina, a beneficiary of the Equity Leaders Programme (ELP), Mary is more than a role model.

Wambui first met Mary after being inducted into the programme, an Equity Bank's paid pre-university internship drive that selects the most academically gifted secondary school graduates from across Kenya and develops them into world-class leaders to transform society.

As part of the programme, beneficiaries give motivational talks to high school students around the country. Mary would occasionally grace such events. Wambui was drawn by how she carried herself as a successful career woman. "I used to see her and think to myself: 'This is such an amazing woman,'" says Wambui.

She had a passion for art and design and would design invitation cards for guests during the events, which she continued to do even after she joined the university. Mary was intrigued by the quality of the design on the cards and asked to meet the person behind it. That is how she ended up getting an invitation to her office at Equity Centre in Nairobi's Upper Hill.

"I was told by the organisers of the event that I was needed at the Equity Centre. I didn't know why because, by that time, I had already left the programme and moved into the construction industry as an intern", says Wambui.

At their brief meeting, Mary expressed appreciation for Wambui's work, praising her for her creativity. She told her she had a project in Mombasa that she reckoned would benefit from her graphic design skills.

"I was shocked that she noticed my cards, and though she didn't know me she thought I could do more than just the cards", says Wambui of her big break.

She says the encounter transformed her hobby into a career, with Mary also becoming a mentor and a friend.

Wambui says the most striking thing about Mary is her approach to relationships, choosing carefully those she lets into her inner circle.

"She goes the extra mile to intentionally help people find their ultimate true selves," says Wambui.

◆ ●●● ◆

As for Reverend Father Reuben Njagi, a Catholic Missionary Priest with Servants of the Sick (Camillians), he was introduced to Mary's family by his friend Reverend Father John Mwai. Fr Mwai requested him to administer Holy Communion to one of the faithful, Cornelia Matteo, Mary's mother.

"The lady was a very staunch Catholic but was unable to go to church due to sickness and requested a priest to administer Holy Communion every Sunday afternoon at home", recalls Rev Njagi.

"I served the old lady [Holy Communion] for three Sundays without knowing any other member of that family, and on the fourth Sunday, she called her daughter on her phone and requested her to greet the priest who had been bringing Holy Communion to her. I found out that her daughter was Maria Wangari, Group Executive Director, Equity Bank!"

Rev Njagi would later meet Mary in her office, where he shared his passion for helping the sick in his capacity as a Catholic priest. "She was touched by the story I shared with her of a project I was involved in supporting deaf Children in Migori County to access affordable education", says Rev Njagi of the encounter.

"The name of the project is B L Tezza Special School for the Hearing-Impaired Children that was started to provide strategic interventions in the areas of education in 2015 with an initial enrollment of 23 hearing-impaired children and learners with Otitis Media to increase access to basic education for them. By the time I was sharing this with her, the school had 62 children".

That is how Mary joined the project she supports to date.

He credits Mary with most of the milestones the school has achieved over the years, leveraging her social networks to bring on board more sponsors.

"To mention but a few, Lydiah Kiburu [Mary's friend and colleague] helped us equip the school library to be one of the best in the area sub-county. Moran Publishers have also generously donated educational resources worth Sh600,000, improving the learning outcomes of our children", says Rev Njagi, adding that Mary has done all this out of her love for helping others and not for personal recognition.

—•••••—

But if there is anyone who knows Mary intimately, it is her three daughters - Joy, Jacqueline, and Lisa. To them, she is more than a high-flying career woman. She is a mother, a friend and a confidante. Talking to them, one can sense the high esteem in which they hold their mother for her achievements in the corporate world.

But their regard for her in that sense changes the moment she walks through the door of the family home and dons her other hat - that of a mother. At home, she is like any other typical African mother, they say. No matter your age or social standing, you will not be spared a good admonishment if you are in the wrong.

All three of them agree they see traces of their late grandmother, Mary's mother, in her in terms of being a stickler for discipline, although there are nuances in how they met it out, especially when they were younger.

Joy, the oldest of the three, has hazy memories of her childhood in Satellite on the outskirts of Nairobi, growing up in a household that she says was filled with love, with relatives from both her Mum's and dad's families frequent visitors to their home.

From her interactions with her grandmother even at an early age and going by her Mum's stories of her childhood, *cucu*, as they still refer to her, was quite the disciplinarian. She believed in the biblical teaching of "spare the rod, and spoil the child".

According to Joy, while also an advocate of strict discipline, her Mum chose a different approach from her late grandmother. But this is not to say she did not get a few spankings growing up.

"I remember getting one beating with a hanger, which was half-hearted. She needed to instil order, otherwise, the house would have been chaotic", recalls Joy.

You also did not want to be on the receiving end of her "lecturing". "She took a philosophical approach to discipline, away from the cane", she adds. By her admission, Jacqueline regularly incurred her Mum's wrath in the form of one of her famous "lectures", which she says to her were worse than getting a beating.

"Her approach to discipline is different, more like coaching, always trying to guide you on the right path".

Perhaps by virtue of being the lastborn, Lisa does not remember ever getting a physical beating for misbehaving even from her father. She, however, agrees with Jacqueline about being scared of her mother when she is angry.

"She has a way with words and is more open to letting us find our way. She's not one to judge," says Lisa of her Mum's approach to discipline.

The three of them are immensely proud of their mother's achievements, but what they find most striking is not her position and influence in the corporate world. They say they are amazed by her passion for giving back to society through her many causes, such as her sponsorship of the Karungu-BL Tezza Special School for the Deaf in Migori County.

Education is close to her heart, perhaps because of her poor background and having been sponsored for the better part of her schooling. "She's very passionate about youth issues and financial literacy and is keen on seeing young people succeed", notes Lisa. She says her concern for others goes beyond helping people meet their immediate needs to enabling them to become self-sufficient.

Joy, however, notes that not all her efforts pay off, with some of the beneficiaries of her mentorship and sponsorship falling by the wayside or trying to take advantage of her. "There are those who do not always work out, but it does not put her off… there are many success stories of people she has helped", notes Joy.

The success stories include one young woman she took under her wing when she got into the Equity Bank internship programme. She went on to be hired as a legal assistant at the bank before moving to Centum Group as a company secretary at one of the investment firm's subsidiaries. She later went to France for her Master's degree and currently works at the American tech giant Amazon.

"She always has something charitable going on. The word charity doesn't begin to describe her. She loves giving people the tools to be self-sufficient", says Joy.

While regretting their parents' separation and consequent divorce in 2018, all three agree it was for the best that things worked out the way they did. They say they have learnt to enjoy life again as a family and individually.

"Sometimes peace doesn't come easy", says Jacqueline, adding that their Mum is back to her lively old self, always cracking jokes and exhibiting warmth of spirit. The entire experience, they say, has made them appreciate one another more, especially the sacrifices their mother made to raise them to adulthood.

"First, I want to say I love you so much and am grateful you were able to come out of a devastating situation and for being an inspiration", says Joy in her parting shot to her Mum.

"I love you so much, and thanks for being there for us", adds Jacqueline

"Thank you for inspiring me to be better", concludes Lisa.

In Pictures

Tracing my
Heritage

A Journey of Discovery

The Art of Balance

In Pursuit of Purpose

Art of Balance

Reaching out and Lifting others

In their words

About the Author

Mary Wangari is the Group Executive Director of Equity Group Holdings PLC. Before her promotion in 2018, she served as the Group Company Secretary, Corporate & Strategy Director of Equity Bank from 2007-2017. She joined Equity Bank in 2004 as the Head of Corporate Strategy & Head of Legal Services. Equity Bank is the largest retail, commercial bank in East and Central Africa, with 20 million customers. As the Group Executive Director, she is responsible for subsidiary oversight, governance & leadership. She has also been a team leader in the bank on several strategic projects including but not limited to first strategic investment in Equity by Africap Microfinance Fund in 2002; Conversion from Equity Building Society to Commercial bank in 2004; Set up of legal division of the bank; The listing on Nairobi Stock exchange in 2006, Uganda Securities Exchange in 2009 and Rwanda Stock Exchange in 2015; The injection of US$185 million new equity by Helios EB Investors in 2007; The 100% acquisition of Uganda Microfinance Limited by EBL in 2008 among others; Greenfield entries into South Sudan, Rwanda and Tanzania; Negotiation and successful completion of JV between Equity Investment Bank and Exotix on brokerage business; Group restructuring of Equity Bank Limited and set up of a Non- Operating Holding Company in 2014; SPA for purchase and subsequent sale by Equity Group of 25% shareholding in Housing Finance the largest mortgage company in Kenya; Acquisition of 79% shareholding of Procredit bank Congo in 2015 for 45million USD; Loan contracts with various lenders including FMO, IFC, EIB, AFDB, CDB, ResposAbility, Blue Orchard among others totalling USD 750,000,000; Formulation of the Equity 3.0 strategy working with McKinsey Consultants in 2013 to 2014; Equity Bank Congo and Banque Commerciale Du Congo merger in 2020.

She is a seasoned Corporate Executive with over 30 years of experience and a corporate management, strategy, leadership and governance specialist. She is also a dedicated Board member sitting on over ten (10) different Boards of Directors. She is a member of the Women Corporate Directors Kenya Chapter Association, an Association consisting of the most influential businesswomen around the world and which equips women with the requisite skills to become visionary leaders. Mary is passionate about gender diversification and inclusion and is involved in mentorship programmes for young women, career mentorship for professionals, sponsorships for bright but needy students and environmental conservation, among other interests. In 2021 she won the Angaza Award, which recognises purpose-driven, women leaders in Banking and Finance who show exemplary leadership and commitment to the industry. She also emerged as the overall winner of the 2021 Women on Board Award held by the Women on Board Network (WOBN). The WOBN awards aim at recognising exceptional individuals and organisations who show outstanding leadership through promoting and impacting gender diversification and inclusion. Mary was recognised for demonstrating purpose, authenticity, resilience, innovation, and sustainable contribution to economic and social-impact initiatives within the Equity Group and outside.

linkedin.com/in/mary-wangari

Made in the USA
Middletown, DE
11 July 2023

34876367R00080